Angora Rabbit

Angora Rabbits As Pets

Angora Rabbit care, pros and cons, housing, keeping, breeding, diet and health.

By

George Galloway

Table of Contents

Introduction 4

Chapter 1. Understanding Angora rabbits 7

Chapter 2: Owning an Angora rabbit 16

Chapter 3: Breeding Angora rabbits 31

Chapter 4: Habitat of the Angora Rabbit 40

Chapter 5: Bunny proofing the house 47

Chapter 6: Dietary Requirements of the Angora Rabbit 52

Chapter 7: Taking care of the Angora rabbit's health 63

Chapter 8: Training the Angora rabbit 77

Chapter 9. Grooming the Angora rabbit 88

Chapter 10: Showing Angora rabbits 95

Conclusion.. 99

References 101

Introduction

I want to thank you for buying my book. This book will help you to understand everything you need to know about domesticating an Angora rabbit. You will learn all the aspects related to raising the Angora rabbit successfully at home. You will be able to understand the pros and cons, behavior, breeding, basic care, keeping, housing, diet and health issues related to the animal.

Rabbits have always been an owner's dream. They are friendly, calm and look beautiful. People think that the good looks of the rabbit are a good enough reason to domesticate the animal, however the domestication of a bunny has its unique challenges and issues. It is important to understand these challenges.

If you wish to domesticate an Angora rabbit, you should understand the various breeds of the Angora rabbit. This will help you to make a better choice. If you are not ready for the challenges that await you as the caregiver of the Angora rabbit, then you are not ready to domesticate the animal.

If you have already bought or adopted an Angora rabbit, even then you need to understand your pet so that you can take care of him or her. It is important that you understand that owning any pet will have its advantages and disadvantages. You should see whether with all its pros and cons, the animal fits well into your household, as domesticating and taming a pet is not all fun and games, there is a lot of hard work that goes into it. When you bring a pet home, it becomes your responsibility to raise the pet in the best way possible. You have to provide for the pet physically, mentally, emotionally and financially.

It should be noted that whether you keep an Angora rabbit for its invaluable wool or only as a friendly pet in the house, you will have to dedicate a lot of time to the animal. The animal will depend on you for its food and shelter needs, and as the owner and the parent, it is your responsibility to make sure that you provide optimum conditions for the well-being of your pet.

The Angora will need a lot of love and care from your side. Like most pet animals, the Angora rabbit is also prone to various kinds of diseases. As the owner and caregiver, you should attempt to understand these diseases in detail so that you can provide the pet bunny with the right care. When you are looking to maintain the health of your pet Angora rabbit, you should make an attempt to understand the common health issues that the animal faces. This will help you to prepare yourself and also treat your pet well.

It is very important that you take time to understand the various stages in the pet's life. Each stage will demand for different care and methods, so when you take the Angora rabbit home, you should make sure that you understand the needs of the animal at the various stages of its life.

It is important that you are ready to commit before you decide to domesticate the animal. If you are a prospective buyer, understanding of these points will help you to make a wise decision. Before you embark on this journey of raising your pet, it is important to evaluate your resources and make sure that you are ready for the pet. You should also evaluate the practical side of things. It is important that you know that the cost of bringing up an Angora rabbit might be more than the cost you would have to encounter while raising a dog or a cat.

Once you form a relationship with the Angora rabbit, it gets better and easier for you as the caregiver. The pet will grow up to be friendly and adorable and will value the bond as much as you do. This will be good for the pet and also for you as the pet caregiver in the long run.

This book will equip you with all the knowledge that you need to have for the successful domestication of an Angora rabbit. This book will help you understand the basic behaviour and antics of the animal and tips and tricks, which will be a quick guide when you are looking for different ways to have fun with your pet. It is important that a prospective buyer has all the important information regarding the animal.

This book will help you to be a better owner by learning everything about the animal and will help you form an everlasting bond with the pet.

Chapter 1. Understanding Angora rabbits

Rabbits have always been a popular choice for pet enthusiasts around the world. People love rabbits for their playfulness and also their cute looks. There are many breeds of rabbits, and the different breeds are popular for different reasons.

The Angora rabbit is a very popular breed of rabbits. While this type of rabbit is obviously popular for its cute looks, it is also popular for another important reason; its fur. The fur of the Angora rabbit is very smooth, soft and gorgeous and is one of the most unique features of the animal. This makes the animal a popular choice with fiber enthusiasts and artists and also the rabbit lovers. It should be noted here that the wool derived from the Angora's skin is priced at a high value. It is an item of luxury owned by wool enthusiasts and is said to be of a better quality than even sheep's wool.

1. The Origin of the Angora Rabbit

The exact origin of the Angora rabbit is still a topic of debate for Angora rabbit enthusiasts, but it is believed that the presence of these large rabbits was found even in the eighteenth century. Angora rabbits have descended from a breed of rabbit that was of Turkish origin.

Some sailors loved the quality of the wool of these rabbits and found it to be useful to take some of these rabbits back with them to France. It is also known that Angora rabbits came to the United States in the first half of the nineteenth century. The Angora Wooler was the common name of all the breeds of Angora.

In 1939, ARBA took the decision to categorise Angora rabbits as French rabbits. In 1944, the rabbits were further divided into various breeds depending on certain characteristics.

It should also be noted that there are many Angora clubs all around the world. These Angora rabbit clubs have dedicated themselves to the preservation and care of these beautiful rabbits. The National Angora Rabbit Breeders Club is one such club that has dedicated itself to the care of Angora rabbits. It is the national club for the main four breeds of Angora rabbits.

2. Breeds of Angora

There are many breeds of rabbits found across the world. Amongst these breeds, there are four main breeds of Angoras. The American rabbit breeder association has recognized these four breeds as a form of Angora rabbits.

- The Giant Angora
- The Satin Angora
- The French Angora
- The English Angora

The American Fuzzy Lop and the Jersey Wooly are the other types of Angora rabbits that are very popular.

It is important that you understand the various breeds of Angora rabbits well. This will help you to choose the Angora rabbit breed that best suits your needs and requirements as the owner. The Giant Angora, the Satin Angora, the French Angora and the English Angora are relatively larger than the American Fuzzy Lop and the Jersey Wooly. The latter two possess high quality wool, but more rabbits are required to produce same amount of wool.

Giant Angora rabbit

The Giant Angora rabbit evidently has this name due to its size. This breed is the largest of all the breeds of the Angora rabbit. The typical mature Giant Angora rabbit will weigh about 10-12 pounds. These rabbits have a very large, oval head with a very broad forehead. The ears are tasselled and fringed. You can also notice forehead tufts in this breed and prominent cheek furnishings.

Satin Angora rabbit

The Satin Angora rabbit is large in size and out of the four breeds of Angora rabbit, the wool of this breed is the shiniest, hence the name 'Satin Angora'. It should be noted that the quantity of wool produced by the Angora rabbit of this breed is less than what can be produced by other breeds. However, the quality, shine and lustre of the wool is the very best when compared with others. If you are looking for a rabbit that will produce good quantities of shiny wool, then the Satin Angora should be your ideal choice.

French Angora rabbit

The French Angora rabbit has more guard hairs when you compare them to the other Angora breeds. It is also known that this breed has the coarsest wool of all. The French Angora rabbit weighs 7-11 pounds. These rabbits have long and round bodies. They are medium in size and have erect and long ears. The face, ears and front legs are covered with short fur. The other body parts are covered with long, soft fur. This rabbits are found in many colors, and require a lot of grooming.

English Angora rabbit

These look like a ball of fur. The English Angora rabbit is beautiful to look at, but they require a lot of time to groom. The caregiver will have to spend time every day if the quality of the wool is to be maintained. The English Angora rabbit weigh 5-7 pounds. These rabbits have a very thick growth of hair. The thick growth of hair covers most of the face and the ears of the rabbit. The body of the rabbit is also heavily covered with wool. They come in various colors.

Harvesting wool

Angora rabbits are very popular for the quality and quantity of the wool they shed. Harvesting Agora wool is very popular and also very simple. You can harvest the wool of the Angora rabbit by the process of shearing or plucking. Both these processes are equally popular. Though the process is simple, each breed of the Angora will have certain details of harvesting that are specific to it. If you are interested in the harvesting of Angora wool, then it is better if you can take the guidance of an experienced breeder.

Life span of Angora rabbits

A healthy Angora rabbit can live from 7 to over 12 years. It is known that an Angora rabbit that is cared for, groomed well and is kept indoors will have a good life span. The key is to provide them the right environment and nutrition to help them to grow, stay healthy and live longer.

Body types of the Angora rabbits

It is known that different types of Angora rabbits have different body types and sizes. An idea of these body types will help you to understand the structure of Angora rabbits. If you wish to learn the various body types of the Angora rabbits, then the following list will surely help you:

Full arch body type

One of the body types of Angora rabbits is the full arch body type. The full arch body type Angora rabbits are very agile and active. They are inclined to be very energetic. The arch of the rabbit begins at the nape of the neck and continues over the shoulders and the hips in an unbroken and fluid line. This line rounds as it reaches the base of the tail. The ears of the rabbit are erect and the fur is spotted. The side profile can be visibly seen tapering from the hind quarters to the shoulders. Some of the popular breeds of rabbits possessing this body type are the Rhinelander and English spot.

Semi arch body type
Some Angora rabbits possess the semi arch body type. This body type is also called the gentle giant. The shoulders of this body type are lower and the hip is at a higher level. The side profile can be seen to be tapering from the hindquarters to the shoulders. Some of the popular breeds of rabbits possessing this body type are the Flemish giant and the American.

Compact Body type
Compact body type Angora rabbits are smaller in length and are also lighter in weight compared to other Angora rabbits. You can also notice a rise at the top line of these bunnies because the depth of their shoulders is less than the depth of the hips. They appear to be well balanced in their looks. Some of the compact body type rabbits are the mini satin, mini lop, the Havana and the Dutch.

Commercial Body type
This body type is used for production and meat. The rabbits with these body types grow very fast in comparison to other body types. Commercial body type rabbits are equally deep and wide in their appearance. They look similar to the compact body type. Some of the commercial body type rabbits are the Rex, the Satin, the Silver fox, the French lop and the Giant Angora rabbit.

Cylindrical Body type
There is only one rabbit breed that is categorised under the cylindrical body type, which is the Himalayan rabbit. The Himalayan rabbit is small in size. The body of this breed of rabbit is cylindrical and quite similar to the Californian rabbit.

Pros and cons of keeping Angora rabbits

Domesticating an animal is a very big decision and you should be well informed when you are trying to make it. It is always better to equip yourself with the right information. If you wish to hand raise an animal, you should make sure that you understand the characteristics and the requirements of the animal well. When you domesticate the Angora rabbit, you will face many pros and cons on the way.

Take some time to understand the advantages and disadvantages of domesticating the Angora rabbit so that you can take a wise decision. This section will help you understand the pros and cons of keeping an Angora rabbit at home. No matter which breed of Angora rabbit you have, you can expect to face the following pros and cons while domesticating the rabbit.

Pros of keeping an Angora rabbit at home

There are many pros of keeping an Angora rabbit. The lovable and affectionate animal can prove to be a great companion and pet. Here are the pros of raising the Angora rabbit at home (please note that although there are females of this breed, we will refer to them as him for ease):

▪ An angora rabbit is a very intelligent and smart animal. You can easily train him to suit him to your family and living conditions. The rabbit will get accustomed and used to the family very easily and pretty soon.

▪ The rabbit is beautiful to look at. With its coat wool, it looks like a small ball of fur. If you are fond of beautiful looking pets, then the Angora rabbit is definitely the pet for you and your family.

▪ Angora rabbits are very energetic and lively pets. They are very active during the early hours of the morning and evening.

- These animals can be very social and friendly in their nature. They will get along very well with you and your family members.

- Angora rabbits are known to have fun. They are entertaining, but that does not mean that they will not be calm and gentle. If the pet is supervised well, he will always have fun in certain limits.

- Angora rabbits are very sweet and gentle in their nature, but they need to be trained well so that they don't get too mischievous. You will also get to see the calm and composed side of the animal.

- An important point to note here is that their nature will depend on how they are raised. If they are raised to be social, they will be very social. So as a master, it will be your responsibility to ensure that the pet gets a healthy and happy upbringing. You should make sure that they spend a lot of time indoors with family members. This will only help in being more social and affectionate.

- These animals are very funny and entertaining. You can be prepared to have a lot of fun around your Angora rabbit.

- There are many people who domesticate Angora rabbits for their warm and exotic wool. If you are a wool enthusiast, then you will love the Angora wool.

- You can enter your pet Angora into various shows that happen everywhere. These are shows that can help you gain popularity and can help you win also.

- If the Angora rabbit is cared for in the household, they are capable of forming strong emotional bonds. These bonds will last for a life time. You need to spend quality time with your pet to form such strong bonds.

- When you domesticate an Angora rabbit, you will have to worry less about his diet. This is because nowadays many diet mixtures and pellets are available commercially. These food items ensure that the right nutrition is given to your beloved pet.

- If you happen to rescue a young Angora rabbit, the good news is that they can be hand raised. Often when a young animal is rescued, it fails to survive. You would have to be extra careful and cautious while taking care of the kit, but when all the precautions are taken, it is a very much possible task to hand raise a bunny or kit.

- These animals are easy to keep. They don't fall sick that often and lead a healthy life.

- If you have a large number of Angora rabbits, you can earn a lot of money by harvesting and selling wool.

Cons of keeping an Angora rabbit at home
There are many cons of keeping an Angora rabbit, such as:
- Angora rabbits have the tendency to groom themselves. They will lick themselves like cats. This can cause the bunny to swallow some hair or wool. The rabbit is unable to cough this ball of hair, unlike cats. This can lead to a serious health issue called wool block. The hairball remains inside the pet's body in this condition. This can lead to many complications if the condition is not treated on time.

- If the Angora rabbit is not under supervision, he can get very mischievous. The animal will chew at things, even electrical wiring. This can pose a danger to him and others. So, either you should supervise the rabbit or keep him in a place where he does not need supervision and is safe.

- The pet can get stressed and depressed if he is left alone for long durations. You can't leave him in the cage for too long.

- The bunnies love to dig in the ground. In fact, the Angora rabbit will try to dig everywhere. If the pet is left on its own, he might try to dig in your sofas, beds, etc.

- The pet also loves to chew. They can chew at all your furniture and bedding.

- Angora rabbits require a great deal of grooming from their owner. This is because the wool of the pet is very thick. If you don't groom the pet every day, the wool can get entangled and the pet can acquire various problems. If you don't have the time and energy to spend a lot of time of grooming a pet, then the Angora rabbit is not the right pet for you.

- Angora rabbits have the problem of overheating. The body temperature can rise beyond safe limits if proper care is not given. This can happen because of the extremely warm wool of the Angora rabbit.

- The cost that you will incur while buying and raising is more when compared to other pets, such as the dog or cat. If spending too much money is an issue with you, then you will have to think twice before purchasing the animal.

- If you are looking to earn money by harvesting and selling wool, then you should know that you will need to buy many rabbits for that. You will also have to invest a lot of money in their care to earn from them.

Chapter 2: Owning an Angora rabbit

A pet is like a family member. You have to make sure that the animal is taken care of. The animal should be loved in your household. If your family is not welcoming enough for the pet, the animal will lose its sense of being very quickly.

If you wish to own an Angora rabbit or even if you already own one, it is important to understand the basic characteristics of the animal. You should know what you can expect from the animal and what you can't. If the pet does not feel wanted and loved in your home, you will see a decline not just in its behaviour but also its health. This is the last thing that you should do to an animal. An animal deserves love and protection from the family members.

1. Bringing home a healthy pet

There are many challenges that you will face while raising an animal at home. Your pet might face health issues that you would have to take care of, but the last thing you want to do is to bring an unhealthy animal home.

When you get an unhealthy or injured animal, you make the road ahead more difficult. The animal could have health issues that might get worse with time. This only emphasizes the fact that it is extremely important that you get a healthy Angora rabbit to bring home.

Often people get so excited about buying the animal that they forget to do the basic checks that need to be done before bringing the animal to your house. You should definitely do all the checks before you buy the Angora rabbit to avoid any future hassle.

It is always advised to discuss the health and also the history of the animal with the breeder before you buy the animal. A good breeder will not hesitate in sharing with you all the details about the animal.

You should make sure that you understand the various health issues that your future pet has suffered. If you are buying an Angora rabbit that is older in age then it is all the more important to make sure that you understand the history of the animal. Discuss in length about the various issues of the animal.

There are a few checks that you can conduct before you buy the Angora rabbit.

The following checks will help you to make sure that your Angora rabbit is in good health and condition:
▪ To begin with, check the coat of the animal. You should look for any abrasions on the Angora rabbit's skin. His skin should not be bruised.

▪ You should look closely for any injuries on the Angora rabbit. If you find some mark or injury, make sure that you understand the cause. If it is a temporary issue, then it is fine. Discuss it with the breeder to make sure that the mark is not the indication of a serious issue with the Angora rabbit's health.

▪ You should look for any hanging limbs in the animal. This is a clear indication of something being wrong with the animal. A hanging part of the body could mean that the pet is severely injured.

▪ You should also check the animal's eyes. The eyes should not be dull. They should be bright and shiny. This can also be an indication to the animal's current health.

▪ The fur of the Angora rabbit is the index of its health. If the fur is soft and shiny, you can be sure that the animal is healthy. On the other hand, if the fur is not good, the pet has health issues for sure.

▪ Another simple check that you can perform on your rabbit is to check the body temperature of the Angora rabbit. The body temperature should neither be too high or too low. Make sure you discuss the right temperature range with your breeder.

2. Licensing requirements

It is important to understand the licensing rules surrounding Angora rabbits. You should be sure that the laws permit you to hand raise the animal. This is important because the law prohibits the domestication of certain animals. When you are planning to domesticate Angora rabbits, you should understand the licensing laws properly. This would help you to avoid future problems with the law. If you domesticate an animal against the law, the penalty could even include seizure of the animal.

It is important that you understand that although the steps of obtaining the license would essentially be the same in most places, there could be slight variations between various regions. Different regions would have their own regulations. This makes it essential for you to contact the local council of your region.

United States licensing

If you are looking to domesticate an Angora rabbit in the United States of America, you need to understand the licensing rules in the country. You don't need a license in the United States to domesticate an Angora rabbit unless you are using them for research purposes. If you wish to register your Angora rabbit, you will have to contact rabbit clubs. This will allow you to show your Angora rabbit.

It should be noted that all the dealers and breeders that make $600/£459.96 to $1000/£766.62 will have to get a USDA license. The commercial producers who sell the rabbits to pet stores should be licensed under the rules of AWA.

United Kingdom licensing

The Rural Land Protection Act of 1989 is the law of New South Wales that governs the domestication of Angora rabbits. According to the law, anyone who wishes to domesticate more than two rabbits needs to have a license to do so. The law also makes it compulsory to vaccinate the rabbit with the fibroma vaccine.

You can obtain a kit that will define all the conditions to domesticate the Angora rabbit from the NSW office. The kit will also have to have the application form. You can also expect an inspector to visit you and your rabbit to make sure that you adhere to all the rules, so you should make sure that you fulfil all the criteria set by the law.

Things to know before you buy the Angora rabbit

When you decide to domesticate an Angora rabbit, there are many things that you should be looking for. You should know where you can buy the animal from and have the right information about various breeders in your state.

Selecting the right breeder

While you are all excited to buy your new pet, you should also make sure that you select the right breeder to buy the rabbit from. It is as important as buying the right pet. If you choose a wrong breeder, you will only have problems in the future.

It is important that you devote some time to looking for breeders in and around your region. It will pay to talk to other people who might have bought Angora rabbits in your region, as they could help you in deciding on the right breeders.

You should understand the reputation of the breeder before you choose him or her to buy your Angora rabbit from. There are some breeders who are into this profession for the love of Angora rabbits and animals in general. Of course they wish to earn money, but not by compromising their prime duty as a breeder.

On the other hand, you will also find breeders who do this only for the sake of money. Such breeders will not hesitate in providing you with the wrong information about the Angora rabbit to make a few bucks. You need to save yourself from such selfish breeders, and the best way to do this is by doing your homework.

A good breeder will help you to know everything that you need to know about the animal that you intend to buy. S/he will not hide anything related to the health of the animal. As the potential buyer, you should know every little detail about your pet.

It is also important to understand here that a good breeder will make sure that you can provide for the animal. S/he will ask you questions and will make sure that the animal will get a good owner and a good home. There have been cases where breeders have denied permission to prospective owners. A good breeder would always make sure that the animal goes into a safe environment, so if your breeder is asking you questions about how you intend to keep the animal, this is a good sign.

The breeder would want to understand the prime motive behind your buying the Angora rabbit. Is it for the love of the animal or the wool? They would also want to understand if you have the time and energy to devote to the rabbit. The Angora rabbit can be demanding as a pet, and you should make sure that you can provide for him.

Keeping in mind the needs of the Angora rabbit, the breeder from whom you buy the rabbit will give you a set of instructions that will come handy when you are taking care of the rabbit. You should make sure that you understand these instructions well.

List of rescue websites and breeders
It can be a very daunting task for a prospective owner to choose a breeder. You have to make sure that you choose the very best, so that you know that your pet has been in the right hands before you.

Although you can buy from pet stores, the problem with pet stores is that you would not come to know about the history of the rabbit, which is so important to understand the health of the animal. You will also not be able to understand the breeding process and conditions of the animal. These are some important factors in determining the health and the history of the animal.

You have the option of adopting an Angora rabbit or buying it from a reputed breeder. There are some factors that will govern the final choice that you make. You should make sure that you understand these factors, so that you can make the right choice for yourself as the owner of a new pet.

If you are looking to bring an older Angora to your home, then you should try to go for adoption. You can help a rabbit get a new home. Many rabbits are mistreated and abandoned by their owners and you can help to give one of these abandoned rabbits a new home.

If you are looking at the financial side of things, you can benefit from adopting the rabbit. You can often expect to get a cage and other accessories with the abandoned rabbit. This will save you from building or buying a new cage for the animal. On the other hand, if you are looking to hand raise a young rabbit, it is advised that you buy from a breeder.

If you are looking for a list of the various reputed breeders, the following list can help you:

- Rabbit haven: https://therabbithaven.org
- Rabbit breeders: http://rabbitbreeders.us
- Evergreen farm: www.evergreenfarm.biz
- Friends of rabbits: www.friendsofrabbits.org

Note: at the time of printing, all the websites below were working. As the internet changes rapidly, some sites might no longer be live when you read this book. That is, of course, out of our control.

Number of Angora rabbits you can keep
Just because you like an animal does not mean that you can keep tens of the same type together. Many a times, there are restrictions involved in keeping the same breed of animals together. It is important that you invest some time to understand these restrictions to avoid any future disappointments.

If you are planning to keep more than one Angora rabbit, you should understand their behaviour and space requirements. If you already have an Angora rabbit and are planning to buy more, you need to make sure that the pets can live harmoniously together.

When looking to domesticate more than one Angora rabbit, one of the most important criteria that need to be kept in mind is the space that you would provide the rabbits. The animals need the right amount of space to grow and develop.

If you buy a new Angora rabbit and realize that he can't live harmoniously with the older one, what will you do? Will you just abandon him? This is not a very good idea. It is better to do your homework well before you make a decision.

These animals are known to be very active. You should be able to provide them a space where they can hop around without any constraints. There should be enough space for all the pets. If an animal has to compete with other animals for space, it will only lead to more trouble in the future.

You should understand that as the animals grow, they need more space. If you plan on keeping more than one rabbit, you would have to give them more space when they grow. You should make sure that your house has the provisions for this. The rabbits can get territorial and can fight with each other to establish their territory. You will have to keep a check on the pets to understand their basic behavior and their urge to establish a territory.

There have been reported incidents where more than one Angora rabbit was able to live peacefully and happily in a cage. It will basically boil down to the individual temperaments of the animals.

The age of the Angora rabbits is another factor that you should take into account. It is also known that if the Angora rabbits are introduced to each other at a very young age, there is a chance that they will get along well. The pets will grow together and will discover things together. This will help them to establish a bond amongst themselves.

It has been seen that pets usually get along with pets of their own age. A huge difference in age of rabbits can be a hindrance in their getting along with each other. So, if you are planning to domesticate more than one rabbit, make sure that they fall in the same age group.

No matter how things are looking, you should always keep a close eye on your pets. Never commit the mistake of leaving them on their own. You might not realize but they can harm each other. The first few interactions need to be all the more monitored.

Give the pets some time to know each other. Monitor their behavior when they are away and when they are with each other. This will help you to understand how things are going. If you see things get out of hand, you should make sure that the pets are kept away from each other.

Angora rabbits and other pets
The Angora rabbit is a social and loveable animal. You can expect your Angora rabbit to be friendly towards pets such as dogs or cats. But this is not a rule, so you will have to make sure that the pets are comfortable with each other.

It is very important that each animal in the household is compatible with one another. If the animals are not getting along with one another then this would mean that you can expect chaos and trouble, not just for the animals but also for you and the other family members.

The type of pet is a very important criterion when determining whether the pets will get along or not. The Angora rabbit will definitely get along with another sociable and friendly pet. If it finds the other animal as a threat, then they will not get along.

The age of the various pets is another factor that should be taken into account. It has been seen that pets usually get along with pets of their own age. A huge difference in age of pets can be a hindrance in their getting along with each other. If your Angora rabbit is very young, you should make sure that you save him from bigger animals in the house. These animals might try to hurt the rabbit, and he would be too young to protect himself from any danger coming his way.

If you notice your pets not getting along well with each other, it is important that you don't force them to interact. They should be allowed to interact and bond in a very natural way. In the case where the pets can't get along even after multiple tries, you should keep them away from each other so that no one is harmed in any way.

Angora rabbits and children
There are many people who think that a rabbit is the perfect gift for a child in the house, but before you blindly follow this advice and get your kid an Angora rabbit, you should make sure that you understand how well this will work in your home.

You should know that although Angora rabbits are cute and playful, they can also be very demanding. If you think that a child will be able to handle the pet on his own, then you might be wrong.

An Angora rabbit will need a lot of love and attention. A child's attention span will be less and they will not be able to provide the pet with the love and attention it needs. The Angora rabbit will feel unloved and this will affect his overall growth and development.

When the Angora rabbit is with the kid, it is important that all their interactions are supervised. This is to ensure the safety of the child and also the Angora rabbit.

Taking care of Angora rabbits
Angora rabbits will require lots of love and attention from your side. You will have to dedicate time to their grooming and general care. You should also take time to spend quality time with them.

If you are worried whether the bunny will be able to form emotional bonds in your home or not, then you shouldn't worry too much about it. If you focus on the right things the rest will only follow. You will be surprised to see how loyal and friendly your pet will be towards you. The pet will grow up to be friendly and affectionate.

Like with other pets, once you form a personal bond with the bunny, it gets better and easier for you as the owner. If you bring a young bunny home and spend your time and energy raising him, you will notice that as the animal grows older, it gets very fond of you.

However, it is important to bear in mind that keeping this animal as a pet will not only require emotional resources, but also economic resources.

Costs that you will incur
As a prospective owner, you might be wondering about the costs that you need to be prepared for to domesticate the Angora rabbit. As the owner and parent of the pet, you will have to make attempts to fulfill all the needs of the animal. It is better that you plan these things well in advance. This planning will help you to avoid any kind of

disappointment that you might face when there are some payments that need to be made.

There are basically two kinds of costs that you will be looking to incur, which are as follows:

The one-time costs: One-time costs are the ones that you will have to bear in the beginning when you decide to hand raise an Angora rabbit. This will include the one-time payment that you will give to buy the animal.

There are other purchases that would come under this category, such as the permits and the license fee of the pet, purchasing price of food containers and the price of the enclosure.

The on-going costs: The on-going costs are the ones that you will have to spend each month or once every few months to raise the Angora rabbit. This category includes the costs of the food requirements and health requirements of the pet.

You should work out all these things right in the beginning so that you don't suffer any problems later. Realizing at a later stage that you can't keep the animal and giving it up is never a good idea. You can keep a journal to keep track of the costs.

Cost of an Angora rabbit

The price of the Angora rabbit will depend on where you choose to buy the Angora rabbit from. You can get a rescued rabbit from a rescue center or animal shelter if it is available.

The next choice is to buy one from the breeder. The cost will vary depending on the quality of the Angora rabbit. A very good quality English Angora rabbit bought from a top class breeder will cost you around $175/£134.33.

Depending on your choice of breeder and the choice of Angora rabbit quality, you can expect to spend $50/£38.38 to $250/£191.90 for buying the bunny.

Health costs

It is important to include the cost of healthcare when working on various costs for the pet Angora. This will help you to get an idea on what you can expect to spend on the general upkeep of the pet Angora rabbit. The Angora rabbit does not require any shots or vaccinations, so you don't need to spend any money on that. The only regular medication that the Angoras need is 'papaya enzyme tablets'. These tablets are required to keep the issue of wool block at bay. You can expect to spend about $10/£7.65 on 600 of these tablets. These tablets don't need to be given daily, they can be given twice or thrice a week, so that means 600 tablets will last you a very long time.

You will be relieved to know that the Angora rabbit does not get sick that often. If you take care of the food and hygiene of the bunny, you can save him from many diseases. He will lead a healthy life if you take the necessary precautions.

You should always focus on the health of the Angora rabbit. This is necessary because an unhealthy animal is the breeding ground of many other diseases in the home. Your pet might pass on the diseases to other pets if not treated on time.

You should also be prepared for unexpected costs, such as sudden illness or accidents involving the Angora rabbit. Health care is provided at different prices in different areas, so the veterinarian in your area could be costlier than the veterinarian in the nearby town.

Cost of food

A domesticated Angora rabbit will mostly be fed hay, grass and vegetables. You might also have to include various pellets and supplements to give your pet overall nourishment. It is important that you understand the food requirements of your Angora in the beginning so that you can be prepared on the monetary front.

You should feed about two cups of greens per day to the rabbit. This should cost you around $10/£7.68 per month. You can expect to pay $3/£2.32 to $5/£3.84 for the pellets.

You should make sure that there is enough fiber in the diet of the Angora rabbit. You need to feed timothy hay to the Angora rabbit every day. This should cost you about $3/£2.32 per month.

Cost of hygiene
A pet needs to be clean and hygienic. If you fail at maintaining hygiene levels for your pet, it will only lead to other complications. The basic hygiene of the pet can be maintained by a good quality shampoo and some towels.

There are many owners that insist on litter training. If you wish to litter train your pet Angora rabbit, you will have to buy the required products for the same. You would need to buy paper litter for the bunny because it is safe even when the rabbit ingests it. You will also be required to invest in a good detergent, which could be bleach. This will be needed to clean the cage and all the areas where the Angora rabbit might defecate. You can look at spending $4/£3.07 for the paper litter per month for the pet. The other requirements of shampoo and detergents should not cost you more than $10/£7.66 per month.

Cost of a rabbit cage
The shelter of the animal will be his home, so it is important that you construct the shelter according to the animal's needs. If the pet is not indoors, most likely he will be in his cage. So, it is important to make this one time investment in a way that is best for the Angora rabbit. The cage of the Angora rabbit should be six feet long, two feet wide and two feet deep. If you can provide extra space to the Angora it

would be better. The price of shelter will depend on the type of the shelter. You can expect to spend $20/£15.36 for the cage.

Miscellaneous costs

Although the main costs that you will encounter while raising your pet have already been discussed, there will be some extra things that you will have to take care of. Most of these are one-time costs only.

You will have to spend money to buy stuff such as a grooming comb, litter box, scissors, brush, nail clippers, food bin, water bottle, accessories and toys for the pet. If you think that something needs to be repaired or replaced, you would have to spend money on doing that.

You can expect to spend some $100/£76.58 on these things. The exact amount will depend on the wear and tear and the quality of the products. In order to keep a track of things, you should regularly check the various items in the cage or hutch of the pet bunny.

Angora Rabbit Vaccination

It is known that the Angora rabbits don't get sick very often and it is not necessary to give the bunnies shots or vaccines. However, if you are in UK, the Rural Land Protection Act of 1989 makes it compulsory to vaccinate the rabbit with fibroma vaccine. The veterinarian might also advise the caregivers to give the Angora rabbits a vaccine against Calicivirus. The vaccine against Calicivirus will keep your bunny protected from the diseases caused by mosquitoes and fleas. You should make sure that you consult the veterinarian and follow his advice. Ideally a Calicivirus vaccine is given when the rabbit is about twelve weeks of age. The second vaccine should be given after about four weeks after the first one. The vet might also advice a booster dose for the rabbit that would need to be administered every year.

Angora Rabbit Insurance

This insurance will help you to take care of the veterinarian bills and injury costs. Although the Angora rabbit does not get sick easily, a sudden procedure can cost you thousands of pounds or dollars. If you buy an insurance policy to cover these conditions, you will save yourself a lot of trouble. Depending on the insurance you buy, you can also cover regular clinic visits. There are some companies that will give you discounts on clinic visits.

There are some companies that can help you with Angora rabbit insurance, such as Exotic Direct, Pet Plan, Helpucover and NCI. These companies have different kinds of insurance. You can choose according to your requirements. You can also get a package deal if you are looking to insure more than one Angora rabbit.

When you buy insurance, you have to pay a deductible amount and regular premiums. You will also be required to pay premiums that need to be paid regularly to keep the insurance policy active.

Rabbit insurance can cost you around $8/£6.14 to $20/£15.35 per month. The exact amount will depend on the company that you choose and also on the area where you live.

Chapter 3: Breeding Angora rabbits

As a new or prospective owner of an Angora rabbit, you might be interested in the breeding cycle and procedure of Angora rabbits. Breeding is defined as the process of production of an offspring by mating by male and female adults.

This chapter is meant to clear all your doubts regarding the breeding of Angora rabbits. It is important to understand the breeding patterns of your pet animals. How well you understand the mating patterns of your pet will also determine how well you look after the pet.

It is also known that the mother can sometimes kill the kits one after the other. There are many reasons behind this, for example if she is unable to provide nutrition to the kits. If the kit has a danger of predators, such as wild dogs, even then the mother might decide to kill the kits. It is important that the mother rabbit is kept under observation during her nesting phase.

If your female rabbit tends to kill her young one, you will have to keep the little ones away from her. It is known that if the mother kills more than two of her kits, she should not be allowed to breed again.

1. Mating behavior of the Angora rabbits

You should understand the natural mating behavior of your Angoras. This will help you to do the right thing when breeding them. This chapter is meant to equip you with all the knowledge that you might need for mating your rabbits.

Each animal species has their unique breeding habits and patterns. When you are looking to take care of your pet well, you should lay enough emphasis on understanding its breeding patterns.

The male Angora rabbit gets sexually mature at the age of seven to eight months, while the female Angora gets sexually mature a month earlier.

Baby Angora rabbits are referred to as bunnies or kits. An Angora is able to produce many kits at a single time. These rabbits are known to be very active sexually. Anyone looking to breed rabbits and produce kits will not be disappointed.

It should be understood that rabbits are able to follow one mating cycle with the other in short durations of time. This means that if the mating procedure of the Angora rabbits is not understood and controlled, your house could be flooded with kits.

A good breeder will always encourage you to thoroughly understand the sexual tendencies of your rabbits so as to not commit any mistake in the future. You need to know how often and in what conditions your rabbits can reproduce. In the wild, kits have higher chances of survival in a warm environment. This means that the rabbits enter their mating cycle in warmer temperatures. You can expect the same when the rabbits are domesticated.

When a rabbit is in its natural environment, the extra amount of light during the summers and also spring brings about a change in its body. The male and female rabbits get sexually active during this time. A male rabbit will display changes in his behavior. He will seem more aggressive and restless. This is due to the sex hormones that have become active in his body. This is how you can identify if your male Angora is ready to mate or not.

Another interesting behavioral change that can be noted in the males is that they become more competitive with other male rabbits. The males who are sexually active compete with each other to establish dominance in the group. This is done so that they can impress the female and attract her for mating.

It is known that in the wild, the dominant male Angoras have a good sex life in comparison to the shy ones. When you see your male Angora getting too aggressive and competitive, you should know that he is ready for mating.

When your male rabbit and female rabbit are ready for mating, you should bring the female rabbit to the male rabbit's cage. It should be noted that the opposite should not be done. You should not take the male rabbit to the female rabbit's cage because the female rabbit can get territorial. You might find the female attacking and harming the male instead of mating with him. Once the male rabbit (buck) is able to attract the female rabbit (doe), the mating can begin. During this process, the female will lie down on a level surface on the ground as an invitation to the male rabbit. The female will also lift its tail up.

The male will mount the female rabbit at this time. The male is known to cast a sharp bite on the nape of the female whilst mating, which should last over twenty seconds.

The mating process will end here and the male will release the female at this time. It should also be noted that the male rabbit will have fur in his mouth because of the bite he had cast. He will also lose his consciousness for some time after the entire process is over.

Now the female, if healthy, is pregnant. The gestation period in the female will last for over a month. Once that is over, you can expect your pregnant Angora to give birth to three to eight kits or bunnies.

It should be noted that the newborn kits are hairless and blind. The female is capable of repeating the same process and giving birth to bunnies many times a year, so should be separated from a male for some time after giving birth. People who breed rabbits for wool generally wait for 40-42 days before they rebreed.

2. Nesting

When you are conducting controlled mating at your home, there are many things that you will have to take care of. You should make sure that the male and the female rabbit are in the same cage when they are ready. After they have mated, you should be ready to take care of the doe. It is also important that you take care of the nesting requirements of the rabbits once the mating is over and the female rabbit is pregnant.

The nesting box is a box is where the female rabbit will give birth. You should make sure that the box is big enough to allow the rabbit to be comfortable, as the babies will spend a lot of time there.

You should only place the nesting box in the rabbit cage when the time is right. If you keep it any earlier, the rabbit will try to dig it as if it is digging a burrow. The rabbit might also use the box as a litter box. Make sure that this does not happen.

The kindling is expected after one month of the female getting pregnant, so you should ideally keep the nesting box in the cage of the rabbit on the twenty-eight day after mating has taken place. The female is expected to give birth anytime from the twenty-eight day to the thirty-first day after mating.

You should put some soft pine and hay in the nesting box before keeping it in the cage of the rabbit. This will give a cushion-like structure to the nest and will make the nest box cozy and comfortable.

There is a natural tendency of a female rabbit that is about give birth; she will pull out some hair from under her chin to be used as a cushion for the young ones that are about to arrive.

After the female rabbit gives birth to the bunnies in the nest, she will try to spend most of the time outside the nest. You will see her in the cage, but outside the nest box. The mother will get into the nesting box to feed the young ones. You can expect this to happen at least twice a day.

After three weeks, you will see that the young ones have started coming out of the nest. They will keep hopping in and out of the nest box at this time.

When you notice that the bunnies are spending a good amount of time outside the box, you should remove the box, as the kits don't need it anymore.

3. Raising a baby rabbit

When you bring a pet home, it is more like a new member of the family. It is very important that you take time to understand the various stages in the pet's life, as each stage will demand different care and methods. In case you decide to breed your Angora rabbit, you will face the situation where you will have to take care of a kit. There are many people who buy kits from the breeders who have to face the same situation.

Hand rearing a baby rabbit can be very tricky, but if you pay attention to the details, it will be fun and interesting. You should take care of a few things to make sure that your baby rabbit is taken care of. When a baby rabbit or kit is born, it has no hair and is blind and deaf. You shouldn't be too surprised to see this condition. You can expect the kit to get his first hairs a few days after birth. The kit will open his eyes after approximately ten days after its birth. This is the time when the ears of the kit also start to open.

It should also be noted that body temperature regulation is very important for an Angora rabbit, but a baby rabbit is unable to regulate the temperature of his body. It is only after 7-8 days that you can expect him to do so.

The female rabbit will give birth to about twelve kits at a time. Some can even give birth to more of kits than twelve. A female rabbit will have about eight to ten nipples. This makes it easier for her to feed all her kits.

If, for some reason, a mother is not capable of taking care of the young, then the kits can be given to another female rabbit that is in the same age group as the mother. This should be done in the first few days of kindling, preferably the first three days.

The kits are weaned after about five weeks. Even when they are feeding off the mother, they need to do it twice a day. Each feed time will last for about three to four minutes. If you are hand raising the infant rabbit, then you need to substitute the mother rabbit's milk. When you feed the milk formula to the baby rabbit, you should make sure that the milk is at the temperature of the blood of the infant. This is a very important point. There is a simple formula for the feed that you should be giving your infant bunny. Take half cup of water, half a cup of evaporated milk, one tsp. of cornstarch and one egg yolk and mix everything together. One tablespoon of this formula should be given once or twice a day. The kits will start eating green leaves and grass after fifteen to twenty days of their birth. You can introduce the greens to them at this time along with the milk formula. This will take care of their daily nutritional requirements.

You will have to make sure that the baby rabbit is experiencing the right temperatures. He has to be warm at all times, but make sure that the temperature does not get too hot, as this can also be harmful for the rabbit.
Before you can start feeding your kit, wrap the infant safely in a blanket. This will help to keep the infant warm. You will have to

constantly monitor the temperature so that it does not overheat the infant.

You should keep the infant close to you as much as possible. Your body warmth is also important for the infant to feel safe. When you are feeding him with the bottle, try to keep the blanket or pouch carrying him close to your body.

You can try opening the mouth of the infant with the help of your index finger and thumb when it is time to feed. Make sure that you are as gentle and soft as possible. You can also close his eyes with your hand when you are trying to feed him. These are simple tricks that can help you to feed a baby that is not being very cooperative. It might take some time, but the infant rabbit will become a little settled with time. You will see him being more comfortable and less restless. You should be a little patient and kind with the rabbit.

Another important point that you need to know is that the bottle being used to feed the baby rabbit should never be squeezed when the nipples are in the baby's mouth. When you squeeze the bottle, there could be a rush of milk inside the infant's body. The liquid could even enter the baby's lungs. So, the best way is to let the animal drink at his pace.

The initial phase of trying to nurse the infant can be stressful and challenging for you, but slowly as the days progress, things will get easier. It has been noticed with the infant rabbits that they might take some time to get used to you and the new surroundings. If your infant is rejecting the milk or the milk formula that is being served to him, then there could be another reason than him being uncomfortable in the new surroundings. It is possible that the animal is rejecting it because he feels unsafe.

You should make sure that the water you use to prepare the formula has been cooled after heating it. It should be noted that you should not use cold water because it is not right for the formula. You should also not use boiling water because it can again destroy the mineral content of the formula. A simple way to make use of the water is to boil the water, and then let the boiled water cool down.

When you try to feed the baby rabbit, he might resist the feed or might just reject it completely. This is normal behavior by the kit and you should patiently keep trying. Don't force him, just gently keep trying and finally the kit will take to the milk formula and also the feeding method.

It is known that the young ones can be affected by bowel-related diseases and diseases that directly affect the urinary tract. It will be difficult to control the infection once it starts spreading, and the joey is too young to have any immunity against such diseases. It is important that you look for the first signs of infection. If you see something is wrong, you should make sure that you consult the vet as soon as possible.

While you are feeding the baby rabbit, you should be very particular about the hygiene of the baby and his surroundings. If there is any milk spillage, clean it immediately so that the area does not become a breeding ground for diseases and infections.

There is also a probability that you have rescued the infant from the wild. If you have rescued a litter, then it becomes all the more difficult for you. This is because the infant must be scared and you will have to work on him on an emotional level. The baby rabbit could be trapped or could be in danger of predators. You will have to take into account the condition of the infant when you are making a plan of how to care for your bunny. You should understand the baby Angora rabbit would be very sacred of all the new things coming its way. You have to be well prepared for this.

Be kind and have some empathy towards the baby. Even if it is difficult for you to see the scared kit, you need to be calm. The kit will get better with time and with the care you provide it.

Angora rabbits can grow up to be very good pets if they are loved and cared for in the beginning. This first year is a crucial time because this is when the kit forms intimate bonds with human beings.

You should start introducing simpler solid foods in the baby Angora rabbit's diet after four to six weeks. This will help him to develop his digestive tract before he can start eating the real adult food of the Angora rabbits.

Chapter 4: Habitat of the Angora Rabbit

By now, you would have made a decision whether you want to domesticate an Angora rabbit or not. It should be noted that whether you keep an Angora rabbit for its invaluable wool or only as a friendly pet in the house, you will have to dedicate a lot of time to the animal.

The animal will depend on you for its food and shelter needs. He can't tell you what he needs. As the owner and the parent, it is your responsibility to make sure that you provide optimum conditions for the good well being of your pet.

If you can't provide your pet a habitat that keeps him happy and safe, then you will fail as the parent of the pet. You need to make sure that the pet gets what would make it happy and comfortable. The animal can slip into sadness and depression if his habitat requirements are not met.

This might seem quite new to you. When you think of it, you will realize the importance of a habitat in an animal's life. Imagine being uprooted from your home and being kept in conditions that don't suit your natural ways of living. Wouldn't that create misery in your life?

You should make sure that you have the provisions to keep the animal indoors when required. In addition, a thorough understanding of its living conditions in the natural habitat is necessary so that you can provide him with an environment that best suits its requirements and needs. A comfortable home would mean a happy pet.

1. Understanding the pet's requirements

An Angora rabbit is a very intelligent and smart animal. You can easily train him to suit him to your family and living conditions. The rabbit will get accustomed to the family very easily and quickly.

Because the animal is easy to keep and train you can keep the rabbit indoors most of the time.

If the Angora rabbit is not under supervision, he can get very mischievous. The animal will chew at things, even electrical wiring. This can pose a danger to him and also to others, so either you should supervise the rabbit or keep him in a place where he does not need supervision and is safe.

When you or any other family member is not around, the cage will be very useful so that you can be sure that the rabbit is safe and sound while you are busy. This makes it important to have the provisions for a cage for the animal.

The pet should be used to being in the cage for some part of the day, so that it is easier for him when he has to stay in it. So, make sure that you keep the animal in the cage sometimes. You should understand that the cage would also serve as the resting spot for the pet. The enclosure will keep it safe and will also protect him from various outside dangers. It is only critical that the enclosure is designed in a way so that maximum comfort, protection and security is guaranteed for the rabbit. This chapter will help you to understand how you can build the ideal enclosure for your pet Angora rabbit.

When you bring the Angora rabbit home, you should spend as much time as possible with him. During this time, you should keep it indoors. It is necessary that the rabbit spend as much time as possible with you. It should also be noted that as your pet grows and matures, it needs some extra physical space to grow, play and hop around. In their natural habitat, rabbits are used to a lot of space.

The enclosure also needs to be escape proof. No matter how comfortable the pet is with you, there are some precautions that you will have to take. What if your Angora rabbit decides to escape from a gap in the enclosure? Make sure the enclosure is designed and built keeping in mind this particular point. Even if the rabbit escapes accidentally, you will not be able to find him. To avoid the trouble for you and the poor pet, you should design a safe and escape-proof cage.

The habitat should be kept as real and natural as possible. You can't create a habitat for a fish when you are domesticating a rabbit. There are specific needs for each animal, even for their habitats. It is important that you understand the habitat requirements of the Angora rabbit. The structure and furnishing should resemble his natural habitat to make the animal feel as if it is in its natural home. The enclosure should also be built in a way that is predator proof. You should make an in-depth analysis of the various predators that could attack the pet animal in his enclosure and plan the safety measures keeping in mind the strength of the predators.

You should also focus on the emotional health of the animal. The enclosure should make the pet emotionally safe. He needs to feel comfortable, safe and secure. If you are unable to provide a comfortable home for the Angora rabbit, he will get stressed and worked up. This will show in his health and behavior, so you should make sure that the enclosure gives him the space to de-stress and relax.

As an owner, it is important for you to understand the temperament of your pet Angora rabbit. The Angora rabbit can't be kept captive for too long, as this has a negative effect on him. Even if the cage is very comfortable, make sure you bring him out from time to time. He should be allowed to release his energy by running around. This pent up energy can make him very negative and ferocious. If you have a big house and an extra room, you can designate one room for the pet Angora rabbit. Wherever you keep your rabbit, the room should be spacious and airy.

2. Building the ideal cage for the Angora rabbit

It is very important to design and build the right enclosure for the Angora rabbit. The enclosure will be like a home to the Angora rabbit, so it is very important that the enclosure meets all the requirements.

The ideal cage should be six feet long, two feet tall and two feet wide. These dimensions are the minimum requirements of the Angora rabbit. It is always better to give the rabbit or rabbits a more spacious environment. If you are planning on more pets, then you need more space.

There might be an instance when you would have to isolate your Angora rabbit. Your habitat should also allow you to do so. The isolation could be needed due to some disease or infection that the animal could be suffering from. The isolated area would help the animal to be treated well and he will be able to heal and get better.

A simple trick that you can use to make the animal comfortable with the cage is to instruct the bunny to go inside the cage, but leave the door of the cage open. If you do this, the Angora rabbit will also not feel captive. Let the Angora come out and go inside the cage at will, but make sure that it spends a considerable amount of time in the cage. It is important that the pet is not forced to go into the cage. He should find the cage homely and should go there without a hesitation.

If you are unable to supervise the pet for some reason, then don't make the mistake of keeping the cage door open. You should keep the cage door closed so that the pet stays inside. This is to avoid any unpleasant incidents.
You should always remember that no matter how much you train the Angora rabbit, you can be surprised and shocked by him. He is a playful, chirpy and hyperactive animal and will not leave any chance to create some mischief.

It is extremely important that you clean the cage regularly. A dirty cage will only lead to infections. You should clean the cage and food and water bowls daily.

The outdoor enclosure should be planned and constructed keeping in mind the basic nature of the Angora rabbit. The animal should have fun, but should also be safe and should not get any opportunity to run away from the enclosure. The enclosure needs to be constructed with high quality material. The outer area of your garden and backyard should also be covered. You can look at using the using the chain links that are used to build cyclone fences, as these fences are very strong and durable.

There is a chance that while playing the Angora rabbit's head might get stuck in a gap in the fence. To prevent any such accident, you can install a preventive wire outside the main fence. This will ensure that the Angora rabbit does not get trapped when you are not around. An Angora rabbit is a good climber, so you have to make preventive measures so that the Angora rabbit does not climb out by placing fencing on the top area. The Angora rabbit also loves to dig, so it should also be taken care of that the Angora rabbit cannot dig and eventually escape from the enclosure.

To make things look like his natural habitat, cover the floor with sand, plants, wooden chips and twigs. Your house should have fencing to protect the pet animal from stray animals. The pet should be able to be at peace when in the enclosure and do whatever he wants to do.

3. Building a rabbit hutch

Building a rabbit hutch is one of the most popular choices of owners of Angora rabbits. You can keep one in the backyard, basement or any other area of the house. A rabbit hutch can be defined as a cage for the rabbit that is constructed generally with wood and a wire mesh that surrounds it. Most rabbit hutches have long legs to keep them anywhere. The ones without legs can be placed over tables or other safe surfaces. It is important that you understand that the rabbit hutch is only one option that you have when your pet needs to be kept in a cage like environment. This does not mean that you keep the pet in the hutch and forget about him.

The hutch needs to be easily accessible. You should keep a check on the rabbit from time to time but also allow the pet some time outside the hutch to just walk around. Many cases have been reported in the past where the owners' negligence towards the Angora rabbits caused serious issues in the animals. You can't abandon your rabbit in a comfortable hutch. The pet should be kept indoors as much as possible, but the hutch can be used when you are not around to care for the pet.

You can buy the rabbit hutch or can design it yourself. It is important that it meets all the requirements of the pet animal. To begin with, the hutch needs to be spacious. The animal should have enough space to walk around. You should make sure that the rabbit hutch does not suffocate the rabbit, so it should be airy and well ventilated. You should make sure that the rabbit has access to food and water in the rabbit hutch, therefore you can install a feed hopper and a good watering system. You should also try to make the hutch attractive for the rabbit. He should not feel bored and suffocated in there. Keep some small and interesting toys for the Angora rabbit in the hutch.

You should make sure that the toys don't scare the pet away; they should be inviting and fun for him. This will keep him happy and entertained. You can look at items such as leafy branches, small logs and shrubs as accessories in the cage. Make sure that the toys are durable and non-toxic. If the pet is able to shred the toy, he will swallow the shreds. This is very harmful and will only invite more trouble for the pet. To avoid all these issues, invest your money to buy the right kind of toys. You can also keep a couple of warm blankets inside the cage so that the rabbit can regulate its temperature if cold.

The rabbit hutch should also allow for proper sanitation. Many cases of diseases have been reported in Angora rabbits due to improper sanitation. If you wish to see your pet healthy, you need to make sure that the hutch provides proper sanitation for him.

The rabbit's hutch would need to be cleaned regularly to make sure that there are no disease-carrying bacteria and viruses in there. These are simple things, but critical when it comes to the wellbeing of the pet in the long run.

The food and water systems should also be regularly cleaned. This is very important because if you fail to do so, the rabbit will always be at a risk of some life threatening disease.

Chapter 5: Bunny proofing the house

Your Angora rabbit is a cute and small animal, but if proper precautions are not taken, it can create havoc in your home. It is very important that you learn the simple ways to bunny proof the home. The worst nightmare of any prospective caregiver is when the pet animal creates a mess in the house. When you have a pet at home, you have to ensure that the pet is safe at all times. This is one of your basic responsibilities as the pet owner.

The Angora rabbit will not think twice before charging into unknown territory. The animal is so small that he can easily get himself into problems. This makes it very important that you understand the behavior of your pet very well.

This chapter will discuss the potential dangers to the Angora rabbits and also some simple ways to bunny proof your house. They will help you to avoid mishaps and also keep the Angora rabbit safe at all times.

1. Why should you bunny proof your house?

Many of you might be wondering why it is so important to bunny proof the house. If you fail to bunny proof your house, you might find your pet seriously injuring himself. It is important that you take appropriate steps to bunny proof the home so that you can be sure of its safety when let out of the cage.

You should be very serious about pet proofing your home. Your Angora rabbit could just chew something dangerous and die. If your pet swallows something toxic, you might not even get a chance to take him to the veterinarian and save him. This makes it very important to look for areas of hidden dangers and keep the pet safe. It will chew your rugs and carpets. It will chew on rubber items, though such things are very harmful for him. It is you who needs to make sure that the pet does not chew on the wrong items. It is also important to save your household things from the pet rabbit. You can't let him chew away your favorite carpet or coat. You will have to make sure that your stuff is safe and the pet is safe, too.

The animal is also very fond of digging tunnels. He will try to dig a tunnel or burrow wherever it can. If you don't pay attention, you might find your rabbit chewing and digging your favorite sofa. You should understand that he is an animal and wouldn't know what is right or wrong for him. It is you who is responsible for your pet. You have to take measures to avoid such incidents in your home.

Angora rabbits are also attracted to plants. They will merrily chew on the leaves of various plants, however many house plants are known to be poisonous for the bunny, so they should be hidden.

Rabbits will crawl into any opening they see. For example, the pet might get under the small opening of a fridge or refrigerator. This is very dangerous because the fan of the fridge can harm him. Similarly, washing machines and dishwashers are potential dangers to the animal. The best way to keep your pet animal out of danger is to know where he is and what he is up to. This will mean that you can help him if he has landed himself into some kind of danger. You need to be cautious when you are using store bought detergents and bleaching powder to clean surfaces and washrooms. If they have poisonous and toxic elements, they can be harmful for the bunny. To be on the safer side, you should always rinse the surfaces with excess water. This will make sure that the detergent has been washed off. Make sure that the pet does not have access to such harmful things.

There could be so many things in your house that look non-dangerous, but could be very dangerous for your rabbit. This is the reason that you might have to monitor the pet animal when he is not in his cage.

2. Blocking off dangerous areas
There is no use to cry after the damage has been done. It is always better to take the necessary precautions in the very beginning. You

should understand the various tendencies of the Angora rabbit that can pose harm to him.

It is always a good idea to block off dangerous areas. This will mean that the Angora rabbit will not be able to enter these areas, and you will be able to avoid any kind of mishaps.

You can use good quality barriers to make sure that the Angora rabbit can't reach certain spots and rooms in the house. You should know that an Angora rabbit can jump a long distance, so blocking off areas should be done keeping this in mind. While they can easily jump off bookshelves, they can also squeeze behind one. Puppy pens and baby gates are two options that you can consider while you are looking for ways to block off certain areas of the house. You can easily find them online or from a store.

Make sure that you make a list of all the areas in the house that you want to block from the bunny. You can choose to block a complete room or certain sections. It is a good idea to make sure that the barriers are made of good quality metal. This will ensure that the bunny can't chew on it. The last thing that you would want is the Angora chewing off the barriers that were meant to block him. The barriers should also not have large openings, as bunny could easily get his head stuck.

One particular type of barrier that I would recommend is barriers that have a very strong base of non-toxic plastic. Barriers made of Plexiglas will also serve the purpose. If you wish to make the barrier at your home, then you can use wood.

To keep the rabbit away from the fridge or refrigerator, you can fix cardboard in the opening. This will prevent the pet from entering the opening. Make sure you use a good quality cardboard. You can also keep such barriers in front of various rooms.

If you have recliners in your house, keep them away from the pet. The pet could be severely injured by these reclining chairs. The reclining action and the spring could injure the pet, especially the younger bunnies. To be on the safer side, always check the chair or sofa that you are about to sit on. You don't want to sit on your bunny and injure him. Make sure he is not hiding under tables and sofas before using them.

You should also make sure that all liquid chemicals are far away from the Angora rabbit. If a chemical is in reach of the pet, he might accidently spill it all over him or even drink the chemical accidentally. Make sure that the bottles are always closed. To make sure that nothing of the sort happens, you should make sure that all such supplies are kept in top cabinets where the pet can't reach.

You should also exercise precaution near toilets and washrooms. The Angora rabbit can easily climb toilet seats and cabinets. Just imagine what can happen if the seat is not kept down. The rabbit can slip or jump inside and can get hurt. To avert any such incidents, make sure that he toilet seat is kept down, but most importantly keep the toilet door closed.

The bunny might accidentally swallow the small or shredded pieces. Make sure that the toys that you allow the pet to play with are of good quality. They should be safe for the rabbit and impossible to swallow. Rubber items can also be very dangerous if they are swallowed by the pet animal.

You should make sure that the pet sleeps in his cage. This is for his safety and also for the good of the family members. You can also keep him in the cage when you can't supervise him and his actions.

3. Keeping the Angora away from house plants

You might be shocked to know that many varieties of plants are actually toxic to Angora rabbits. Your rabbit doesn't know this and he mind end up eating the most toxic plants.

Plants such as tulips and holly are extremely toxic for the Angora rabbit. Instead of listing the entire range of house plants that are toxic to your rabbit, I would recommend you looking up the particular plants that you have in your home to see whether they are poisonous or not to your pet. The best thing to do will obviously be to keep the plats in an area where the pet Angora rabbit can't reach them.

If you find your beloved pet chewing on some houseplant, you should stop him from doing so. It is a good idea to take him to the vet immediately to make sure that he is safe and sound.

Chapter 6: Dietary Requirements of the Angora Rabbit

In the wild, Angora rabbits are grazers. As the various seasons change, the grazing capacity of these animals also changes. The food habits of captive bunnies vary slightly from wild bunnies, however we can do our best to provide for their every nutritional need. This section will help you to understand the types of food you can serve to your Angora pet.

There is no denying the fact that the diet is the one of the most important factors that contributes to the growth of an animal. You have to make sure that your pet gets optimum nutrition at all times. This will keep him in the prime of his health.

If your Angora rabbit is well fed, you will see the positive effects in his health, his mood and his general behavior. The kind and type of food that he eats will have an effect on all other aspects of his wellbeing and his life. Taking care of your pet's diet should always be a priority for you. The rabbit will have certain natural inclinations based on his habitat and history. You should make an attempt to understand these natural inclinations, as this will help you plan his food.

If your pet is eating tasty and nutritious food, he will be healthy, disease free, stress free and happy. So, it is important that you make all the efforts to make sure that the pet is getting his daily dose of nutrition and health. This is your responsibility as the owner of the pet.

1. Nutritional requirements of the Angora rabbit

The Angora rabbit needs a diet that is rich in protein and fiber. The rabbits need the high amounts of protein to supplement the growth of wool. You can see a decrease in the quantity and quality of wool in an Angora rabbit who is not fed high amounts of proteins. Along with the high amount of protein, the diet should also contain good amounts of fiber. The high amounts of fiber will help in saving the Angora rabbit from wool block. The fiber is also good for the general digestion of the animal. Sometimes, the rabbit can swallow some hair by mistake. The fiber in the diet of the pet will help him to avoid any harmful consequences because of the swallowing of the hair.

In the wild, these animals would generally feed on hay and grass, so the food that you should serve to your pet bunny should mainly consist of hay, grass, oat hay and timothy hay. The pet Angora should also be served green leaves as a part of his diet. The ideal food of the pet would consist of a generous helping of dark green leaves along with good amount of hay or timothy.

To give the Angora rabbit optimal nutrition, you should also serve him pellets that are commercially available. This will help him to get all rounded nutrition. Some owners also add sunflower seeds to rabbit food because this is good for digestion. Angora rabbits can be given these pellets to give them a good supply of nutrients. These nutrients will help in the overall growth of the pet.

If you are looking to buy commercial pellets to supplement the diet of the Angora rabbit, then you should make sure that the commercial pellets have about 17-20 per cent of protein in them. These pellets should also contain good amounts of fiber in them. Make sure that you check the percentage of both the protein and fiber in the commercial pellets before deciding to give them to your pet rabbit. You can easily buy the commercial pellets and other supplements online or from local feed stores and pet shops.

It should be noted that you should always introduce new foods and fruits to the Angora as early as possible. If the pet is young, it is easier for him to acquire the taste. If you serve vegetables and fruits along with the green leaves, hay and pellets to the Angora rabbit, you can be sure that your pet is getting the required nutrition from his food.

Another important point when deciding and finally buying the various food types for your pet is that a pet is totally dependent on you for its needs. It won't be able to tell you that the food is good or bad in quality. As the chief caregiver of the pet Angora rabbit, it is your duty to make sure that the food is of the highest quality. You should avoid buying any low quality food just to save some amounts of money.

If you are looking for food options, then the following foods can be introduced in the diet of your beloved pet:

- **Grass:** Rabbits love their grass. This is what they feed on in the wild. If you leave them in a garden, they will happily graze on the grass. Grass would be your most natural choice of primary food for your pet Angora rabbit.

- **Grains:** You can include grains in the diet of the pet bunny, as this will add to the quality of the food. Grains are known to be very healthy. They are as good for Angora rabbits as for human beings. You should make sure that the grain that you serve the pet with is not sweetened and is natural. There are many kinds of grains that you can include in the diet of the pet bunny, such as wheat, milo, oats, millet and barley. These grains can be bought easily from a local store. They will surely make the food of your pet tastier and healthier.

- **Carrots:** You can introduce carrots in the pet's diet. The best way to serve them is in their natural form. The carrot is easy to feed and also easy to eat. Carrots are juicy vegetables and have a good content of water. They will also provide the necessary fiber to the Angora.

- **Sweet potatoes**: You should always try to keep the diet of the Angora as natural as possible. It is always better to give the animal some vegetables. The pet will enjoy these vegetables, and in addition to that they will be very healthy. Sweet potato is a great option for this.

- **Apples:** You can also serve fruit to your pet. It is known that Angora rabbits enjoy eating certain fruits, such as apples. You can give the bunny apple leaves, fruit and twigs. You can also serve cut fruits or small fruit to the pet animal. If you don't want to serve apples everyday then you can alternate them with some other food types. Fruit is tasty and has many nutrients. This will have a positive effect on the health of the pet animal. It should be noted that you should remove the seeds of the fruits before serving them to the Angora rabbit.

- **Melons:** You can also serve melons to your Angora rabbit. You can these fruits into small pieces before serving them to the rabbit, so that it is easier for the pet to chew. This will have a positive benefit of the health of the pet animal. It should be noted that these fruit types have very high sugar content. This can be harmful for the Angora, so make sure that you give these fruits to the Angora rabbit in limited quantities. It should be noted that you should remove the seeds of the fruits before serving them to the Angora rabbit

- **Alder:** You can also serve alder to the pet. If you don't want to serve them every day you can alternate them with some other food type. This food type is inherently juicy and has a good water content. This will also provide the necessary fiber to the pet rabbit.

- **Asparagus:** You can also serve asparagus celery to the Angora rabbit. If you don't want to serve this food type every day then you can alternate them with some other food type.

- **Basil:** You can introduce basil in the pet's diet. The best way to serve it is its natural form.

- **Cilantro:** You can include cilantro in the diet to add to the quality of the food, as it is known to be very healthy. This food type has a good water content.

- **Wild rye, wild lettuce, mint, horse nettle, grapes leaves and vines, catnip, broccoli leaves, beet tops:** I've put these together because it is important to note that these can be given to your pet, but in small quantities. It is known that grass and hay are the chief food required for the Angora rabbit. When we talk about hay, we are mainly talking about alfalfa hay and timothy hay. Alfalfa hay is known to have high amounts of fiber in it. The hay should be dry, but should also be soft. Soft and dry hay is the perfect meal for the Angora rabbit. It is good for the gums of the animal and is also good for the digestive tract and stomach of the animal. You will have to watch for sharp pieces in the dried grass or hay. The sharp pieces can hurt the gums and inner lining of the mouth. If such pieces are swallowed, they can harm the digestive tract and the stomach of the pet.

2. The amount of food Angora rabbits require

As the caregiver of the Angora rabbit, you might want to give all the love and food that you can to your pet. While it is okay to shower the pet with love, feeding too much food is not healthy. You should limit the quantity of food that you serve to the pet. This section will help you to understand the right amounts of food that your Angora needs.

You should also note that the rabbit will need different quantities at different stages of his life. A growing bunny's requirements will be different from the requirements of the adult bunny. Similarly, a pregnant or lactating mother doe will have different requirements.

The breed of the Angora rabbit will also directly affect the food that he should be eating. The size of the rabbit will also be a factor that would need to be considered. It should be noted that an Angora rabbit belonging to a larger breed will typically need about six to eight ounces of food in a day. On the other hand, smaller ones will need three to five.

There are many food types you can choose from, but make sure that you don't serve all the food types on a single day. You will have to mix and match to create the right balance, though there are certain food types that the pet requires daily.

If the Angora rabbit is served more food than he requires for a healthy wellbeing, he will rapidly gain weight. It is important to note that obesity in Angora rabbits is the major cause of some serious health problems.
An obese Angora rabbit will have difficulty mating. It is known that obesity drastically reduces the ability to reproduce in Angora rabbits. Not only will the bunny face issues in reproducing, but the health of the pet will also suffer. It is known that an obese pet is likely to live fewer years compared to a healthy and fit Angora rabbit.

It is important that the everyday diet of the Angora is able provide it with all the necessary nutrients. As mentioned before, the Angora rabbit needs good amounts of fiber and protein in its diet. The deficiency of various nutrients can lead to many diseases in the Angora rabbit, so it is important that the food items that are served to the Angora rabbit are rich protein and fiber.

It is important that you keep track of what you are feeding your Angora rabbit throughout the day. Keep a check on all the vegetables and fruit items that you are serving to the Angora rabbit. You should discuss the exact amount of food that the animal needs from time to time with the veterinarian.

3. Foods to avoid
There are many food types that are not suitable for your Angora rabbit. You will have to be very careful when you are planning the

diet for your pet Angora. A good diet will help to keep the pet animal healthy and will also protect him from various diseases.

Sometimes, you may want to give your rabbit the same food you are eating, but this can prove to be very fatal for the Angora rabbit. He can suffer serious consequences. It is important that you keep a check on what the kids are doing with the pet animal. It is always advised to let the children interact with the Angora rabbit under an adult's supervision.

Keep the food of the Angora rabbit fresh, simple and healthy. When you are giving fruits, then you should make sure that it should not have seeds because the seeds can be poisonous for the pet Angora rabbit.

If you are looking for a comprehensive list of food items that are unhealthy for the Angora rabbit, then this list will help you. You should avoid these food items:

▪ **Caffeine**: You should keep caffeine such as tea and coffee away from your beloved pet. Caffeine can cause nausea, diarrhea and other health issues in the Angora.

▪ **Chocolate and cocoa beans:** These items are unhealthy for Angora rabbits, especially for the younger ones. These items can cause extreme restlessness in the pet and can also lead to complications. You should make sure that you keep these food items away from the Angora.

▪ **Onion and garlic**: These items are unhealthy for Angora rabbits. You should make sure that you keep these food items away from the Angora.

▪ **Avocado:** Another food item that is dangerous for the Angora rabbit is the avocado. The digestive system of the animal is not suited to digest this food item. The animal will experience diarrhea and vomiting after it consumes this food. The animal might also encounter difficulties in breathing because of this food item.

- **Cookies, cakes and candy:** These items are unhealthy for Angora rabbits. You should make sure that you keep these food items away from the Angora.

- **Dairy products:** Dairy products can cause vomiting and body weakness in the pet bunny. In some extreme cases, the pet might also suffer from tremors.

- **Raisins and nuts**: Another food group that is dangerous for the Angora rabbits are raisins and nuts, especially walnuts. You might believe that nuts are healthy foods, so they should be fine for your bunny, but this is not true. The digestive system of the bunny is not able to digest nuts. If a bunny consumes them, he will experience vomiting and body weakness. Raisins can negatively affect the kidneys of the Angoras. If these food items are given for a longer duration, substantial damage is done to the kidneys.

- **Mushrooms:** Mushrooms are unhealthy for Angora rabbits. They can render a lot of harmful effects on the animal. You should make sure that you keep these food items away from the Angora.

- **Pits and iceberg lettuce:** This is another food type that is dangerous for Angora rabbits. The digestive system of Angora rabbits is not suited to digest them, so you should always avoid feeding them to the bunnies.

- **Tomatoes**

- **Tulips and other flowers.**

In case of a situation where the Angora rabbit has consumed something toxic, you should consult the veterinarian as soon as possible. You should not delay matters like these.

4. Water needs of the bunny

An Angora rabbit needs good amounts of water for its survival. You should make sure that the animal always has access to drinking water. Water helps the Angora rabbit to regulate its body temperature due to its thick coat.

If the Angora rabbit is not hydrated well, he can develop severe health complications. You can even lose your pet Angora because of lack of water in his system. To avoid such incidences, make sure that the pet is hydrated at all times.

You should buy chew proof water bottles for the Angora rabbits. These bottles can be easily hung in the hutch or cage of the rabbit and are readily available.

If you keep a water container in the hutch or cage of the pet Angora, there is a high probability that the pet will play in the water. Even if he does not play, the water can spill easily in the cage or over the Angora rabbit. The water can wet the coat of the Angora rabbit, and it is important that the wool of the Angora rabbit is always dry. Wet wool is the source of many health issues, especially skin-related diseases in the Angora. The water bottle will allow the pet to easily drink water and will also keep the wool of the pet dry.
You should make sure that there is water in the water bottle at all times. You should re-fill the water daily and should also clean the bottle frequently. These are simple way to keep the pet bunny healthy and hydrated.

It is easy to clean these water bottles. There are special brushes available in pet stores and online that will allow you to clean the water bottles easily and without a fuss. Make sure that you clean them at least once a week. You should also make sure that you purchase the right extensions to attach to the water bottle. These extensions will allow you to keep the water bottles in place and will also allow you to fix them at the right angle in the cage of the pet bunny.

If you stay at a place where water freezes during winters, you will have to take special care of the Angora rabbit. Such a condition can force the pet to go without water for extended periods, which is extremely dangerous for the Angora. A simple solution to this problem is to use heated bowls in winter. However, with this the same issue of the wool getting wet arises. You will have to be more careful and will have to make sure that the fur of the pet is trimmed regularly. The trimming will reduce the chances of skin issues because of wet wool. You should try your best to keep the Angora rabbit safe and dry.

5. Introducing new foods to the Angora rabbits

When you bring a pet Angora rabbit home, one of the biggest concerns that you will have is regarding its diet. It would take you time to understand the diet preferences of the new bunny.

If you want to introduce new foods or switch foods, you can't suddenly change the rabbit's usual meal plan. It is suggested that the pet be introduced to different food types quite early in his life. This will make it easier for you and also for the pet Angora rabbit.

In case a certain food item is not available, you know that you have other choices. If you don't introduce new foods to the pet Angora, he will turn out to be a very fussy eater and you will find it very difficult to provide him with the right types of food. You should slowly introduce new foods to the pet Angora. There are some simple tips and tricks that you should be following to make sure that the pet is eating well even when new foods are being introduced.

You should introduce one new food at a time. A simple way of introducing new food in the diet of the Angora rabbit is by starting out with a small amount of the food. Take a bowl and add the usual food of the pet in it.

Now, take a very small amount of the new food that you wish to feed your pet and place it in the bowl. Mix the contents and serve the food to the pet animal. You should introduce vegetables and fruits in the diet of the Angora rabbit. You should remember that the Angora rabbit needs time to get used to it, but there is nothing to worry about even if the pet leaves the new food in the beginning.

Just keep adding a very small amount of the food item in the usual food of the pet. This might take some time, so be prepared. Once you see that the pet has started easting the new food along with the usual old food, you can gradually increase the portion of the new food.

The given process will take some days, but you will have to have some patience. The idea is to help the pet get used to the food before you can expect the pet to eat it. Once he is gets used to it, he will try out the food item on his own.

Chapter 7: Taking care of the Angora rabbit's health

An unhealthy pet can be a nightmare for any owner. The last thing that you As the prospective owner or the owner of a beautiful Angora rabbit, you might be thinking about what you can do to ensure that the pet is always in the prime of its health. You can contribute a great deal to the health of the animal.

The food that you provide the animal with, the conditions that you keep him in and the love that you give him will all affect the general wellbeing and the health of the Angora rabbit.

You should always make sure that your pet is kept in a clean environment. A neat and clean environment will help you to ward off many common ailments and diseases. In addition, make sure that the pet is well fed at all times.

When you are looking to maintain the health of your pet Angora rabbit, you should make an attempt to understand the common health issues that the animal faces. This will help you to prepare yourself and also treat your pet well. It is important that you take care of your pet's health. The pet will depend on you for most of its needs. It will not be able to tell you if it is facing any discomfort regarding its health. You should be able to identify the symptoms of various diseases in your pet to treat it well.

You should also be able to diagnose any symptoms of injuries in your pet. If you treat him in your home, then you should do it very carefully. In case you have any doubts, you should take the pet to the veterinarian.

1. Injuries in Angora rabbits

As you would have understood by now, your Angora rabbit is a very mischievous animal. He will lead a very active lifestyle, which will make it susceptible to many injuries. If your pet injures itself, you should be able to diagnose the injuries so that they can be treated well.

Never commit the mistake of ignoring an injury or symptom. Even if you have the slightest doubt, you should always act on it. It is always a good idea to take the Angora rabbit to the veterinarian if you spot something unnatural with the pet.

You should be on the lookout of any symptoms that your Angora rabbit might display when it is injured. These symptoms could mean that there is something wrong with your bunny. It is important that you understand that your pet animal might not show any signs of injuries. It will be your responsibility to diagnose the injury before it turns into a bigger problem.

Is your pet looking very lazy and lethargic? Is your Angora rabbit looking very disturbed? This could be because he has injured himself and is in pain. The limbs of the animal could also be hanging. This is also a clear sign of injury in the pet. You should closely examine his limbs to be sure.

Is your pet stumbling? Is the pet showing uncoordinated movements? If you find these symptoms, then you know that the pet has some issues. Take him on your lap and gently check his limbs. If there is a change in the way he sits or stands or carries himself, this could also mean that the injury has forced the pet to change the way he usually is. This could be because he is in pain.

You should look out for the feces of the animal. If there is any change in the color of the feces, this could mean that there is something wrong with the health of the pet.

Do you witness any changes in the skin of the pet? If yes, then this could also mean that there is something that needs your attention. Don't overlook anything that does not seem very natural.

Do you spot any blood on the skin of the animal? Does the fur of the pet look different? You should look for bloodstains in the enclosure of the animal also. This could mean that something is not right.

A sick Angora rabbit will seem very lethargic. The animal will show a drastic change in its activity level. It will not let you come close to him and will get irritated. The pet might show violent movements. He might get stressed when someone approaches him. The pet would be seen grinding its teeth tightly and flicking its ears or shaking its head angrily. You would be able to make out that something is wrong with the pet.

He would make strange and loud noises from his mouth when not grinding his teeth tightly. If you measure the body temperature of the animal, there will be a change in the body temperature of the animal.

The Angora will lose an interest in eating and drinking. This is a sign that something is definitely wrong with the pet.

Look for certain common symptoms, such as coughing and vomiting. If your pet looks scared and tense, you should understand that it is for a reason. You need to closely examine him to find out what is wrong. This examination will help you to understand if there is something wrong with your pet.

While you are examining your pet, you should also understand that your pet could be scared. It is important that you make the pet feel comfortable. This will help you conduct the examination properly and without any problems.

To make sure that the pet animal is not terrified when you are trying to examine him for any potential injuries, you should make sure that you conduct the examination in a closed area, a place where the animal feels safe and protected. You should try to examine him indoors.

Make sure that all the tools that are needed for the examination are ready. You shouldn't leave your pet alone to fetch the tools. Everything should be ready before the examination.

The noise level around you should be as low as possible. The noise will stress the pet out and will irritate him, so make sure there is no noise around. Conduct the examination in a quiet place. This is important to keep things under control.

Do not let the place be crowded when the examination is being conducted. Make sure that all the other pets and your family members are outside and not in the same place where the examination is being conducted. If the animal sees you being fidgety, it will only add to his stress. Be as gentle and kind as possible. You should in no way add to the stress and pain of the pet.

You should be as calm and as confident as possible. Your confidence will give him some hope and relief. These are some very simple tips, but will go a long way in ensuring that the pet is being handled well.

You should check his entire body. Remember to check on both sides of the body. Start the examination at one particular point and then move ahead from that point. The examination should be definite and guided and not random.

Look at how your pet responds to the body examination being done. If you feel that the animal is not taking it too well, you should stop the examination. You should look for any stress signs that he displays. It is important that you don't ignore any symptoms. It is also important that you don't force anything on the pet; otherwise the animal can go into deep shock. After your initial check-up, if you find something wrong then visit the veterinarian.

You should never self-treat the pet. This could complicate things further. Take the pet to the veterinarian because s/he is the best judge of the pet's condition. Discuss your doubts and confusions with the vet.

2. Common health problems in Angora rabbits

Nobody would want to see a helpless animal suffering from a disease. To make sure that your bunny enjoys good health at all times, it is important that you recognize the symptoms of diseases that can affect an Angora rabbit at an early stage.

If you can detect a disease at an early stage, there are more chances that the disease will be cured. To be able to do so, you should make an attempt to understand the various diseases that can affect an Angora rabbit along with their symptoms.

There are many common health issues that your Angora rabbit is prone to. There are many issues that might not start as a big problem, but become serious problems if not treated on time.

You should also never ignore any symptoms that you see because an ignored symptom will lead to serious problems later. As in humans, an early-detected problem or disease can be treated easily in pets. It should be noted that even if your pet is healthy and all seems to be just fine with him, you should make sure that you take him to vet for periodic visits. This is to make sure that all remains fine.

The vet will examine the health of the pet Angora rabbit, and will help you to understand if something needs your attention. Such visits will also help in detecting even the slightest issues with the bunny. There are many diseases that might not start with a big warning but might become serious diseases if not treated on time.

This section will help you to understand the various common health problems that your pet bunny can suffer from.

Coccidiosis

One of the most common health problems in Angora rabbits is Coccidiosis. Protozoa Cocci, which have one single cell, cause this particular health problem.

It is important to know that there are nine types of Cocci that can affect rabbits. Eight out of these nine types are known to affect the intestines of the bunnies. The ninth type of Cocci can affect the liver of the Angora rabbit.

You should also know that cats, dogs and chickens can also be affected by Cocci. It is also important to note that young rabbits are often more susceptible to Cocci, so they need more attention and protection.

The older bunnies have immunity against this disease, so if you have a young Angora rabbit, you should be worried about this health issue. It is important that you understand the causes and ways to avoid this disease.

One of the most common causes of this disease is unclean area. If the cage or the hutch of the rabbit is not cleaned for days, you can expect your Angora rabbit to get infected with this disease. The parasite will dwell in dirty areas. The Angora rabbit will ingest the egg of the disease, causing a parasite. They will do so when they lick or eat from dirty cage floors or when they eat contaminated hay.

While the adult rabbit is less likely to suffer from this condition, it can be a carrier. It can shed the eggs of the parasite in its feces. This can further infect other pet Angora rabbits in the vicinity. The eggs of this disease causing parasite can thrive and survive for over a year in a humid and warm place. This makes it all the more important that you regularly clean the surroundings of the Angora rabbit.

Symptoms:

You can look out for the following symptoms in the bunny to know if he is suffering from this particular disease:

- The pet will lose his appetite. You will find him avoiding even his favorite foods. He will not drink water, which could further lead to dehydration.

- You will notice a sudden and drastic weight loss in the pet. This is one of the most common symptoms of this condition.

- Another symptom of this disorder is vomiting.

- The pet would be seen struggling during his bowel movements. You should watch out for this symptom.

- You will notice the bunny to be very lazy and lethargic.

- You can spot your Angora rabbit sitting in one corner with a hunched back. His feet will be forward, and he will appear to be really sad and sick.

- The pet will suffer from diarrhea. You might also notice blood in the stools of the Angora rabbit.

Treatment:

If you find any of the above symptoms in an Angora rabbit, it is important that you waste no time and take the pet to the veterinarian. The vet will conduct some tests to confirm the condition.

The most common treatment of this condition includes the use of corid powder, which you can buy at a pet store. Sulfamethoxide is also used to help the pet recover from this condition. It should be mixed with water and given to the rabbit for seven days. After the first cycle, a break of over seven days is taken. After that, the mix needs to be given for another seven days.

Most veterinarians will suggest completing these two cycles at least once in six months. This ensures that the Angora rabbit does not get this health condition. This is all the more important in young bunnies. If your female bunny is pregnant, you should not administer this particular drug to the doe. It can be given to her once she is in the lactating phase. Usually the symptoms of this disease start with the pet being lazy and losing its appetite. The other symptoms might not show for a very long time. The best way to avoid this disease is to take the necessary precautions.

It is important that you don't ignore any symptom and consult the vet as soon as possible. Always try to maintain cleanliness in the hutch of the pet Angora rabbit.

Ringworm
Ringworms are a very common issue that can affect your pet rabbit. Ringworms can attach themselves to the Angora rabbit, which will cause immense discomfort.

While many people don't consider this a major health issue, ringworm should never be ignored. They are known to be very dangerous and can be a potential threat to your other pets also as well. You should make sure that ringworms are treated well and on time.

If you believe that ringworm is a worm, you are wrong. It is a fungus and fungal treatment is required to get rid of ringworm. If you are treating your pet for worms, you will not be able to combat this condition. The problem with this disease is that it can get worse with time, so it is important that you treat it as soon as possible. If the ringworms are allowed to grow on the animal, they will lead to a lot of fur loss. There are many causes that could be behind the ringworms attacking your pet. One of the most common causes of ringworm is contact with infested animals.

Ringworms can easily travel from one carrier to another. So, if an animal infested with ringworm comes into contact with your Angora, he can easily get it too.

Symptoms:

You should be on the lookout of the following symptoms to confirm the presence of ringworm in your Angora rabbit:

- Your rabbit will scratch itself often.
- He will be irritable and uneasy.
- Ringworm makes the animal itchy and too much itchiness can develop red sores on the body. You should be on the lookout for such obvious symptoms of ringworm.
- The pet will slowly develop bald patches. You should be on the lookout for this symptom. It is one of the most common symptoms of the Angora rabbit being infected with ringworm.
- The head of the Angora is most likely to be affected. It will slowly spread to other parts of the body. You should look out for bald patches on the head.

Treatment:

If you find the given symptoms on your pet then you can be convinced that your pet has been infested with ringworm. It is important that you take the steps to help your pet get rid of them. If you do not treat the pet soon, they will only trouble the poor animal more. You can successfully treat the ringworms using an antifungal treatment for the disease.

You should not allow the pet to come into contact with other pets. The ringworms can spread very easily and human beings can also easily catch them. You should wear gloves when you go near the pet Angora.

Snuffles

Another common disease that can affect your Angora rabbit is Snuffles. This condition is characterized by excessive sneezing, a running nose and running eyes in Angora rabbits. This disease is caused by a bacterium called pasteurella. The bacteria affect the respiratory system of the Angora rabbit.

This disease is basically caused by an infection in the nasal area and the tear ducts. It is a difficult and contagious disease. It is better to take measures to prevent the disease rather than treating at a worse stage. It is highly advised that a potential rabbit owner selects a healthy Angora rabbit. If the rabbit has a runny nose, it is better not to buy him. If you are breeding Angora rabbits, it is important that all the quarantine and sanitation procedures are strictly followed. Another common cause of this health condition in bunnies is stress. When your pet is going through excessive stress, it will lead to a nasal infection. You should try your best to ensure that the bunny is not under any stress. Make sure that he has a good habitat. You should make sure that you provide your bunny with healthy diet and optimal hygiene conditions.

Symptoms:

There are certain symptoms that will help you to diagnose whether your pet animal has the disease snuffles or not. In case you find the symptoms, you should make it a point to take your pet to the veterinarian. It should be noted that snuffles is a contagious disease. It is important to treat it in time; else it can spread to other rabbits. In severe cases, all the infected animals have to be killed to save the other bunnies from the disease.

The following symptoms will help you to confirm whether your pet is suffering from this health condition:
- One of the early symptoms of this disease includes running eyes and running nose. If your pet is showing fidgety movements and seems to have a shaky head, then the pet could be suffering from this disease.

- The pet will show a significant reduction in his weight. If you observe closely, you will be able to hear a startling sound as the rabbit breathes.

- As the disease advances, the bunny will become very lethargic. His immune system will be affected. He will lose interest in his regular activities.

Treatment:

If your pet is suffering from this disease, you would have to take certain measures to help the bunny get better. It is advised to administer Tetracycline to the animal. You can mix it in the food of the rabbit. You should also make sure that the pet is given a very healthy diet. Make sure that all the necessary nutrients are given to the pet along with the doses of Tetracycline. This is an ideal solution in the early stages of the disease.

You should continue the doses for about 20 days, depending on the condition of the bunny. Even if the symptoms of the disease begin to disappear, you should complete the treatment to avoid any future infection. It is often seen that the disease causing bacteria continue to reside in the nasal passage of the bunny. It should be noted that in advanced stages, the bunny will have to be taken to the lab for identification of symptoms and further treatment.

Salmonellosis

The Salmonella bacteria is said to affect Angora rabbits and cause this condition, also called scours. This condition is characterized by excessive diarrhea in Angora rabbits.

The main reasons behind this condition are unhealthy diet and poor hygiene conditions. If you give your bunny a proper and healthy diet and also try to maintain optimal hygiene conditions around him, you can definitely avoid this health condition in the pet. If the pet animal is suffering from a severe case of viral or bacterial infection, scours could be one of the side effects of the infection. In such cases, it is best to treat the infection if you want to treat this condition.

If you feed excessive food to your pet, much of the food can go undigested. This will hamper his digestive system and bowel movements. One of the effects is scours. Another common cause of this health condition in bunnies is stress and over-heating. When your pet is going through excessive stress, it will lead to scours.

Symptoms:

There are certain symptoms that will help you to diagnose whether your pet animal has this particular disease or not. In case you find the symptoms, you should make it a point to treat his condition well. You can also take your pet to the vet.

The following symptoms will help you to confirm whether your pet is suffering from this health condition:
• One of the early symptoms of this disease includes diarrhea. If your pet is suffering from diarrhea that you are not able to control, then your pet could be suffering from scours.

• You should keep a check on the stools of the rabbit. The color and texture of the stools will help you determine whether the rabbit has Salmonellosis or not.

Treatment:

If your pet is suffering from Salmonellosis, you would have to take certain measures to solve this issue. It is advised to administer probiotics to the animal. He should also be given electrolytes. The electrolytes will help to give the body the salts that it might have lost because of the condition.

Once your pet starts getting better, you should make sure that it is given a very healthy diet, as a good diet prevents Salmonellosis. Make sure that all the necessary nutrients are given to the pet. You can also look to give him supplements if his diet does not provide the right nutrition. You can even consult your veterinarian if your pet doesn't get better.

Pneumonia
The Angora rabbit is also highly susceptible to pneumonia, especially when the bunny is young. If your Angora shows symptoms of a respiratory disorder, then you should look for the various symptoms of this disease. This disease can be caused by bacteria of a virus that thrives in dirty and unsanitary conditions. This is the reason why it is always advised to keep the hutches clean and sanitary.

The main cause of this health condition is damp hutches and cages. If the living conditions of the pet are not good, he can suffer from this disease.

It is important that you treat this disease because it is known to be a life threating condition. If you discover any respiratory disorders in your pet, you should take the issue seriously because as the disease reaches its advanced stages, it becomes more difficult to treat.

Symptoms:
You should be on the lookout for the following symptoms to confirm the presence of the disease in your Angora rabbit:
- If your pet animal refuses to eat, this could be because of this disease. The pet will suffer a drastic loss of appetite.

- Is your pet being very lazy and lethargic? Is he refusing to move? This could also be because of this disease.

- The pet Angora will have difficulty breathing. There could be a blockage or congestion in the chest area. This is a very common symptom and should be taken very seriously.

- The pet could be suffering from a high temperature. This is also a very common symptom accompanying pneumonia.

- The pet might vomit the food that he is fed. This is because of the congestion in his chest.

Treatment:

There is treatment available if your Angora rabbit is suffering from pneumonia. The type of treatment that will be chosen will depend on a few factors. If the pneumonia is too severe, then a different treatment is chosen in comparison to if it is not too severe.

The vet will recommend antibiotics to combat the disease. The dose and strength of the antibiotic will depend on the severity of pneumonia in the pet bunny. If the bunny is not able to recover and is already at an advanced stage, the dose of antibiotic is injected directly through the skin. This is known to work rapidly on the animal.

Chapter 8: Training the Angora rabbit

When you decide to keep an Angora rabbit as a pet, you should understand that Angora rabbits are smart and intelligent animals. You will find it easier to train them to stay in a household. By nature, animals can be unpredictable. Therefore, efforts and planning at your end are important. This training phase will also require you to be patient. You will have to do a few trial and errors before you can be sure that your pet is well trained.

It is very important to train the animal to make him more suitable to a household. You should remember to have fun even during the training phase. You shouldn't be too harsh on your pet. Give him some time and show some patience and he will get there before you know. The most important point that you need to remember when you are training your pet is that it is not possible to train the Angora rabbit in just a few steps. The bunny will forget and go back to his basic habits if you are not consistent.

You will have to do the same steps again and again. These repetitive actions will require patience and time. It may take weeks or months before you see any positive results. If you don't see instant results, don't get angry, and don't hit the animal. Pets are like small children. You have to deal with them with patience and love. If you beat your bunny out of frustration, you will rupture the bond between the two of you. He will detest coming to you and things will only get worse. If you think that punishing the pet will help to train him, then you should understand that the pet might not even realize which actions are leading to the punishment. It will only confuse him further. When you hit him, there is a great chance that he will be physically hurt, so you can also injure the pet severely. The pet might slip into sadness and depression if severe training sessions continue. This will hamper the pet's emotional bond with you and also his health. You should refrain from doing so.

When you are training the pet, try not to chase him. Rabbits generally associate chasing with being held captive. If you wish to play with them, kneel on the floor. You should be on the same level as the rabbit if you wish him to enjoy playing with you. They will play in your arms for some time and then will want to come down. You should be prepared for such behavior from your pet. Let him be the way he wishes to be. This will allow him to get comfortable in your presence.

The training phase can be a great opportunity for you to learn more about your little pet. No matter how much you read about an animal, your pet will have some individual characteristics that will separate him from the rest of the lot. This is a good time to learn about all these properties.

1. Is it possible to train an Angora rabbit?

You would definitely want the pet to be well trained and behaved. The Angora rabbit is used to being in the wild on its own. If you wish to domesticate it, you have to tame it. If you wish to tame it, you will have to rely on some training skills to do so. This is a simple way to monitor their behavior and to teach them what behavior is acceptable and what isn't. You should adopt simple training techniques to train your Angora rabbit. If you are consistent, you will get very good results.

Many of you might be wondering whether an Angora rabbit can actually be trained if he is so mischievous and playful. The truth is that they can be trained. You will be required to put in more time and effort to do so.

You should not make the mistake of starting the training of the Angora rabbit when he is too old. The sooner you start the training, the better it is. You should start the training when the rabbit is very young. In fact, you should start the training soon after you bring him home. You should understand the importance of training the pet animal. The Angora needs to be taught certain things so that it does not get back to his basic wild behavior. Apart from teaching him the right behavior, training will also help to form a bond between you and your pet. It will bring the two of you closer to each other.

If you start the training the pet from a young age then this will give the pet some time to learn and understand what is expected of him. It is also important that the training is not stopped at any stage. Once you see him picking it up, reduce the intensity but don't stop the training. Your Angora rabbit can be trained for many things, such as bath training and litter training. Training the pet is an important part of bringing up a pet in the household. This is a simple way of helping him adapt to your home and your family.

When you are looking at training the Angora rabbit, you should be aiming for litter training and training against chewing and biting above everything else. These trainings are important to help the bunny adjust into the household and also to make things easier for you and your family. While you are training your pet, you should remember that the Angora rabbit needs to feel comfortable and secure in your presence. You should spend quality time with him. Don't put him in the cage unnecessarily.

If he is left in the cage unattended all the time, he will become very aggressive. This will encourage his chewing and biting behavior. Always remember that they can bite when they are scared and disappointed. You should never neglect your pet. The Angora rabbit will learn slowly, but you have to be compassionate and kind towards the pet. Treat him when he exhibits good behavior. This will encourage him further.

Litter training
To begin with, you should buy a few litter boxes. Keep these boxes in various areas of the house where the Angora rabbit is most likely to litter. You should signal the Angora rabbit by pointing towards the litter box.

The pet should slowly realize that he needs to use the box if he wants to get out of the cage. You should wait near the cage until he is all done. You should cover the various corners where you have found the litter earlier. In addition, install one box in the cage. Eventually, you want the Angora rabbit to litter in the cage itself. If he does not go in the box, whenever you see him relieving himself carry him quickly to the box during the act. He will soon realize that if he wants to go he will have to do it in certain spots.

If you notice that the pet is not using the litter box installed in his cage, then you need to understand why. There is a chance that the litter box is uncomfortable for him. In such a case, you should look to buy a comfortable litter box.

Another point that you need to understand here is that Angora rabbits are very smart. When the Angora rabbit understands that you will let him out of the cage once he uses the litter box, he might pretend to use it. You need to check the box and make sure that he has actually used it. The Angora rabbit will take its own time to adjust with the environment. It is always difficult for a new pet to adjust. If you get him a new cage or if you make any changes to his surroundings, he will find it difficult to adjust. However, this problem is only time related and will get solved. Every time the Angora rabbit litters outside the box, place his litter in the box that he should be using.

You need to show the pet that he should be using the litter box. This could be difficult for you in the beginning, but the Angora rabbit will learn soon. You should place food and toys in areas and corners that you want to save.
You can also place a mat underneath the litter box to save your carpet or floor. Make sure that the mat that you use is waterproof. The litter box of the Angora rabbit should definitely be kept clean to maintain overall hygiene and to prevent diseases. You should wash the box once a week.

Observe your Angora rabbit's mannerisms when he is using the litter box. If he has a tendency to bite the mat underneath or stuff kept around, you should discourage this behavior. To do so, you can use bitter food sprays on the mats and other items. This will automatically discourage the pet from biting around when he is littering.

You should leave some organic paper litter in the box to encourage the pet to use the box again. This is a simple trick that you can use when you are trying to litter train your pet. This paper litter can be bought very easily. You can cover the litter with some hay. When you are buying a litter box, you should remember that the size of the box will depend on the size of your Angora rabbit.

If you are domesticating more than one Angora rabbit in your home, this will also affect the littering process of the Angora rabbits. This may come as a surprise to you, but the dominant pet could affect how the other pets use the litter boxes in the house. You might notice that the habits of a dominant pet Angora rabbit are influencing the other pet Angora rabbits. The dominant one will always try to boss others around and make them feel inferior.

You should make sure that each Angora rabbit has its own box so that he not left to use the carpets and the floors. Even after you have trained your Angora rabbit to use the litter box, you have to be vigilant. There could be instances when your pet Angora rabbit would suddenly give up the use of the litter box. Instead of getting angry at him, it is important that you probe into the reason for his sudden change in behavior.

When the Angora rabbit is sick, he might give up use of the litter box. The main reason behind this is that the pet might not have the strength in his hind legs to get on to the box. He could be suffering from a disease, which could make him weak and lethargic. You should be cautious when you observe such changes in your pet Angora rabbit. Don't ignore his condition, or don't force him to use the litter box.

You should not get angry at the pet because he is littering on the floor. It is not his fault if he is not well. The best thing to do in such a situation is to take the pet to the vet. This will avoid the condition to get worse. He will look for the symptoms of various diseases and will help you to understand what is wrong with the pet.

Training the pet against chewing and biting

When you buy a new Angora rabbit, you might notice that the animal has a tendency to bite things. This is very natural behavior. They try to bite and chew everything, so you shouldn't be very surprised. He will not even hesitate to chew wires, which can be very harmful for him. This is the reason why the rabbit needs to be supervised. As an owner, this can be uncomfortable and worrisome for you. However, you should know that this is absolutely normal for the bunny and that you can slowly train the Angora rabbit not to exhibit such behavior. You can teach him not to bite you and other members.

The first thing you should remember is that you should not harm the pet when he tries to bite you. This could scare him and will make things worse for you. The pet needs to be handled with care if you wish to teach him the right behavior in the household.

If you mishandle the pet and try to beat him, he might also try to bite you and harm you. Avoid going down this road and aim at training the Angora rabbit well. It is important that you understand that reason behind the Angora rabbit's biting. More often than not, Angora rabbits do so when they are in a playful mood. If the Angora rabbit wants you to play with him, he could just signal you to do so by chewing. Such behavior is quite common in younger Angora rabbits. Another reason behind an Angora rabbit's nipping is that the animal could be scared. When you bring the pet to your home for the first time, everything around him will be new. It is quite natural for the pet to get scared. This is the reason that chewing and biting is very common in a new pet Angora rabbit. Give him space, time and also your understanding.

The Angora rabbit might be happy and playful, but his chewing and biting will hurt you, so it is important to train him against such kind of behavior.

As explained earlier, an Angora rabbit can exhibit such behavior when they are scared. It should be noted that if the Angora rabbit has had a history of abuse, then you can expect him to chew and bite more in fear than in a playful mood.

Don't worry because this is a passing phase. The love and warmth he will get at your place will help him to come out of his history of beatings and abuse. If the pet is very young, he needs to be taught the behavior that is expected of him. He needs to learn to be sociable. He needs to learn that it is not okay to bite people. There are some tips and tricks that will help you to teach him all this.

Every time the pet tries to bite you, you should loudly say the word 'no'. Do it each time until the Angora rabbit starts relating the word 'no' to something that he can't do. Don't beat him because this will only scare him. Just be stern with your words and actions.

If you think that the above trick is not very useful, then you can put the pet in his cage for some time. The pet will eventually understand that this behavior will send him into the cage. The word 'no' and the act of putting him into the cage will make the pet more cautious of his behavior.

It should be noted that it will take some time for the Angora rabbit to understand this. Until then just be patient and keep repeating these actions each time he tries to nip you. The Angora rabbit will call back on his memory eventually and relate the cage to something punishable. Another trick to help the Angora rabbit understand that he can't nip and bite is to hold him and drag him away from you. You need to establish the fact that you are the dominant one in the house. When you are pulling the Angora rabbit away, you need to be very careful. You want to train the pet and not harm him. Use your thumb and the index finger to hold the skin at the back of the Angora rabbit's neck. This skin is loose and you will be able to hold easily.

There is another trick that can definitely help your training sessions with the Angora rabbit. You can apply something bitter on your toes and fingers, so that when the Angora rabbit bites you, he gets that bitter taste. When he tastes something bitter and terrible on you, he will eventually give up on nipping you. It is important that the food item that you use is bitter but is not harmful for the Angora rabbit. You should know that there are some specially designed bitter foods for Angora rabbits.

You can buy various bitter products, such as bitter apple and bitter lemon.
These products are extremely safe for the Angora rabbit, so you can use them without any doubts. They render the bitter taste that will disgust the Angora rabbit.

While you are working hard to train your pet Angora rabbit well, you should remember that you don't want to do anything that is not right for the pet in the long run. For example, if you use too much of these bitter food products, the digestive system of the Angora rabbit can get upset. You just need to spray a little. This will be enough to get the job done and also not affect the Angora rabbit in a negative way.
After your pet has tasted the bitter product and is disgusted, you need to make it up to him. Wash off your hands and toes nicely and give the pet a treat. This is important so that the pet is not scared of you and your hands. This will also make him realize that nipping is not accepted, but eating from your hands is.

You can also introduce clicker training as a part of training the Angora rabbit. Clicker training is a process in which a sound or click is made to let the pet know that something is expected from him. The association of a sound and an action will help the rabbit to learn faster.

You can buy a clicker from a pet store, or you can use any simple item can produce some noise. For example, you can make some sound from your mouth or can use the sound of a pen to train the pet bunny. With continuous training, he will understand what action he should perform.

You can also reward the Angora rabbit with his favourite treat every time he does a good job. This will motivate the Angora rabbit to exhibit a good behaviour. It is also important that the bunny is not punished because that will only send negative signals to his brain. It is advised that you combine clicker training and litter training to make your pet bunny litter in the litter box.

2. Fun tricks and games with Angora rabbits

As the prospective owner of the Angora rabbit, you will be delighted to know that you can teach your pet Angora rabbit some fun games and tricks.

The way you can train your Angora rabbit for various essential behaviors, you can also train them to understand some tricks. For example, the animal can be trained to know that he is being called.

You can teach him to associate certain actions with certain words. There are many other fun tricks that will help you bond with your pet. These tricks are also very entertaining. Your family and friends will surely have a great time when you and your pet do your fun tricks.

Like any other training, even these fun tricks will take some time. You will have to be patient with your pet if you want him to understand your commands well. There are some easy and fun tips that will make this process entertaining.

You can teach to roll on the floor. Similarly, you can teach him to run around your feet. You can give a healthy treat to the pet when he is able to follow your instructions. The idea is to repeat a set of instructions and help him do an action. Give him a treat when he does it right. This will help him to understand what is required. Treats are a simple way of making the pets do what you want them to do.

In the beginning, you will have to repeat the set of instructions again and again, but with the passage of time, your aim should be to reduce the number of times the instructions need to be repeated.

The pet bunny should be able to associate a set of words to an action. You should also not make him too dependent on the treats. It can be very difficult if the bunny hides and refuses to budge. Don't force him and give him some time. Angora rabbits will follow your lead and will have fun with you, but you need to be a little patient with them.

A simple trick that you can try to make your pet bunny listen to you is to give him a special treat. All animals love treats.

Stand up
When sees this favorite food item in your hand, he will get all excited. When you bring the treat near him, take the treat upwards. The Angora rabbit will try to reach the treat, and in this process will stand on its hind legs. Next, lower the treat towards the ground. The movement of the treat in your hand will also inspire the movement of the bunny. Do it every time you give him the treat. The Angora rabbit will slowly realize that to eat the treat he will have to stand on the hind legs and then sit back.

Make sure you do this only for fun and not to trouble your pet Angora rabbit. Once you and your pet do the trick well, you can flaunt and boast in front of your family and friends that you can make the pet perform tricks.

Roll over
Lay the pet Angora bunny on the ground, say the words roll over loud and clear and then give the pet a gentle roll over with your palm. Repeat this action many times. This will teach the pet that he needs to

roll over. The pet will start associating the word roll over with a roll over on the ground. When you say roll over, he will start rolling over on the ground on his own. This might take many days, even weeks of practice, so be prepared.

If your pet seems uncomfortable with you rolling him over, you should just quit. Some bunnies might feel a little vulnerable with such an action. Understand your bunny's reactions and then take the next step.

These tricks and games can be very entertaining for everybody who gets to watch them. Angora rabbits are very entertaining and when you apply these simple tricks with them, they become more playful.

Chapter 9. Grooming the Angora rabbit

If you are domesticating the Angora rabbit for its wool or for showing, it is very important that you groom the pet well. Grooming the pet rabbit is also necessary to maintain the hygiene and wellbeing of the pet. Even if the pet will not participate in shows, you should make sure that he is neat and clean at all times.

When you are looking at grooming sessions for your Angora rabbit, you should pay special attention to the coat of the rabbit. This chapter will help you to understand the various dos and don'ts while grooming your pet Angora rabbit.

It should be noted here that the Angora rabbit will require frequent bathing. This is important to keep the wool in good condition. If you fail to groom the pet regularly, you will put the wool and the skin of the pet at risk. When you decide to keep an Angora rabbit as a pet, you should understand that you will have to pay attention to the basic cleaning and grooming of the pet bunny.

You should start the grooming sessions with the pet when he is very young. When you start a grooming session with the adult Angora rabbit, he might take some time to get used to the new routine. On the other hand, if you start when the pet is very young, you give him some time to get accustomed to frequent grooming sessions. This is good for you and the pet in the long run.

You should take special care of the Angora rabbit's wool. The wool needs to be combed regularly to maintain its health and luster. If you don't comb it regularly, the wool will be tangled. Once the wool is tangled, it can be a real pain for you to get rid of these tangles. You will have to apply pressure and force, which can be very uncomfortable and painful for the pet Angora rabbit.

It is important to note that this can cause the bunny to shed loose tendril of its wool. This is a warning sign for you as the caregiver of the pet that something is not right with the health of the Angora rabbit. Angora rabbits have the tendency to groom themselves. They will lick themselves like cats. This can cause the bunny to swallow some of the hair or wool. The rabbit is unable to cough up this ball of hair, unlike cats.

This can lead to a serious health issue called wool block. The hairball remains inside the pet's body in this condition. This can lead to many complications if the condition is not treated on time. The Angora rabbit feels that his stomach is full because of the presence of a hairball in his stomach. This makes him to lose his appetite and he eats less. This can be really detrimental to the overall health of the pet Angora rabbit.

You should help your pet in this condition by feeding large quantities of hay because this contains fiber. You should also make sure that the pet Angora rabbit drinks a lot of water to help him during this condition.

1. Bathing the Angora rabbit

An angora rabbit requires frequent bathing. It might be a difficult task for you to bathe your pet, but this is no way means that it is okay for the bunnies to go without bathing. It is important that you schedule time for dedicated grooming and bathing of the Angora rabbit.

If the pet is not clean, he will attract fleas and other parasites. This only means extra work for you and veterinarian visits for the Angora rabbit. Make sure that the pet is well groomed to avoid other hassle.

To prevent the Angora rabbit from getting sick, make sure that the bunny is bathed every now and then. The frequency would depend on the climate and the environment of the bunny. If it is too hot or if the surroundings are not too clean, it means that your pet should be given a bath more often. Bathing is also important to keep the coat of the Angora rabbit clean. This is important to maintain good quality wool. If you don't clean the coat, the rabbit gets prone to many skin diseases. If the Angora rabbit is shedding its wool tendrils, the excess wool might stick on its the body. When you give the pet a bath, the loose tendrils will just get washed off with water. This also means that the fur will not be shed all over the house.

When you are looking to give a nice bath to your Angora rabbit, you should be looking at two things: a good quality and mild shampoo and a few towels. It is very important that you choose the right shampoo for the Angora rabbit.

If the shampoo is too harsh, it will leave rashes on the Angora rabbit and might even cause serious damage to his skin. This makes it important that you invest in buying a mild shampoo. You can easily get a good quality shampoo online or in the pet store. Make sure that the shampoo that you choose is very mild on the skin and has proven to be ideal for the Angora rabbit.

You can take a small amount of shampoo and test it on a small part of the skin of the Angora rabbit. This is to make sure that the shampoo is safe for the pet. If you see the skin reacting, you should make sure that you avoid this shampoo.

You also need a few towels handy for the Angora rabbit. They will help to dry the wool of the pet nicely. While one will be used to dry the water off, the others are required to cover the floor.

The calm nature of the pet will make it easier for you to bathe him. However, there are a few precautions that you need to take. You should understand that how your rabbit behaves in water will depend on its individual personality. It is important that you make a few attempts to understand your pet's personality. Don't give up and understand his behavior and mannerisms. This will only help you in your future dealings with the pet.

If your Angora rabbit is suffering from ringworm infestation, you will have to use a shampoo that can help the Angora rabbit to get rid of the ringworm. You should consult a veterinarian before you use a specialized shampoo. It is important not to take a chance on the health of the Angora rabbit.

When you are ready to give the Angora rabbit a bath, you should make sure that the water you are using to bathe the pet is warm. Make sure that the water is not too hot. You can also keep it in the garden area. Make sure the surroundings are not too dusty and dirty. Lift your pet animal delicately in your hands. Make sure that your grip is firm. To make sure that your grip is strong, place your hands on the stomach area and hold him firmly.

Place the Angora rabbit in the tub of warm water for a few seconds. Observe how he responds to water. If you see him enjoying, then your work becomes easier. You can also sprinkle water over the Angora rabbit.

Take him out of the water and put some shampoo on his back. You should form a good lather with your hands from the ears towards the tail region. Make sure that the pet does not escape when you are shampooing it. You need to have a firm grip on him. You need to make sure that the entire coat of the Angora rabbit is cleaned nicely. This is important so that the wool can be combed easily after the bath is done. You can also make use of the kitchen sink to give the Angora rabbit a bath.

Another way to bathe the bunny is to sway him under running warm water. Turn the tap on and make sure the water is warm. It should not be cold or too hot. Once you are convinced that the temperature of the water is right for the pet, hold the pet and bring him under the water for a few seconds.

Take him away from the water after a few seconds. Now apply some shampoo over the Angora rabbit. Keep swaying him under the water until all the shampoo is washed off. It is very important that all the shampoo is washed off. If there are shampoo residues on the pet's skin the skin will become damaged and will show signs of rashes and abrasions. While you are bathing the Angora rabbit, it is important that you protect his face. Water should not enter his eyes or ears. These are sensitive areas and water could cause some damage to them.

Keep him on the towels and use another towel to pat him dry. Make sure that he is absolutely dry before you let him go, otherwise dust and dirt will stick to his wool.

Once the pet Angora rabbit is dry, you should comb the wool of the bunny very nicely. This is important so that you avoid any tangles. Once the tangles are formed, it will be very difficult to get rid of them. You can also give him treats during the bathing session because you will be spending a lot of time bathing him. Though the pet is calm, he might get all worked up and fidgety after some time. You can expect to spend about thirty to forty minutes in one bathing session with the Angora rabbit. It should be noted that when the pet is shedding wool, the time will increase. You can expect to spend about forty to sixty minutes in one bathing session.

2. Grooming nails, ears and teeth

The ears of the Angora rabbit need to be cleaned regularly to prevent wax build up. There are many owners who might not consider ear cleaning an important part of grooming, but in reality wax can lead to infections.

In severe cases, the hearing of the pet can be compromised. It is important that you know the early signs of infestation. It is important to see the veterinarian in case you have a doubt about infestation. Don't put any drops in the pet's ears without consulting the vet. In general, you should try to clean an Angora rabbit's ears once a week, or at least once every ten days.

You will require a cotton swab and an ear cleaning solution that will be easily available either online or at the store. If there is somebody in the house who could help you, it will be easier to clean the ears. Sit comfortably on the floor and hold the bunny. Use your lap to give support to the bunny's legs. Take a cotton swab and apply some cleaning agent to it. You should use the cotton swab with the cleaning agent to clean the parts of the ear that are easily visible to you. Don't go too deep because this can hurt the Angora rabbit. You should definitely not try to go further in the ear canal. Repeat the process on both the ears.

The bunny might get uneasy and might try to get away from your grip. To make sure that the Angora is stable and not jerking, you can give him a treat. This will keep the rabbit occupied and will make your job easier.

It is also important to cut the nails of Angora rabbits regularly. You should be looking at doing so at least once a month. This is a part of the overall grooming of the pet Angora rabbit.

You should also make sure that you use the right equipment to cut the nails of the pet Angora rabbit. You should use good quality animal nail clippers. Along with that, you would need soap and styptic powder in case you cut too far and he bleeds.

If there is someone else in the house, you can ask them to hold the rabbit. Place the pet animal in your lap in a way that he is comfortable and you have access to his nails. If the nails of the bunny are not cut on a regular basis, there is a chance that the nails will get stuck somewhere. You can imagine the pain your bunny will have to go through if the nails are uprooted. You will have to rush to the veterinarian to help the bunny. Not only this, but the long nails can also leave marks and scratches on your skin. So, make it a point to cut the nails of the pet regularly.

As a rule, you should try to clean the bunny's teeth regularly. If you ignore his teeth, you will only invite unwanted problems for the pet Angora rabbit. You will notice tartar depositing on the teeth if they are not clean. This will automatically lead to tooth decay. Start by placing your finger in his mouth for periods of time, and then after a while place a toothbrush or your finger with rabbit toothpaste on it to brush the teeth. Please do not use human toothpaste.

Chapter 10: Showing Angora rabbits

There are many owners that keep and domesticate Angora rabbits for the specific purpose of making them take part in shows. These shows are extensively popular amongst many rabbit lovers. If you also wish to keep or domesticate the rabbit for the purpose of showing, then you need to make sure that you follow certain guidelines. The American rabbit breeders association has set some guidelines that will help you to prepare your Angora to participate in such shows. You should make sure that you understand these guidelines. These guidelines will help you not just in preparing your Angora rabbit for the show, but also to take good care of the pet. You will understand how to keep the pet in its best form. Listing these guidelines is beyond the scope of this book, but do look them up if you would like to compete.

1. Preparing your Angora rabbit for the show

If you want to enter a show with your Angora rabbit, you will have to make sure that your rabbit is in its best form. You should take care of the health and wellbeing of the animal and make sure that he is ready for the contest.

After you are sure that your Angora is ready to take part in the contest, you can plan on getting him admitted. You need to be a member of an organization that will help you to compete.

The ARBA organization and BRC organization are the two organizations that will allow you to be a member and also enter a show with your Angora rabbit.

The process to become a member is fairly simple and straightforward. You need to approach the organization and show an interest in being their member. You should also register your pet Angora under your name.

Once you are a member of the organization, you will be intimated with all the latest happenings and shows in your area. You should be alert regarding the requirements and deadlines.

Always keep checks on the shows happening in your area. You should check if your Angora fits the requirements. When you find a show that allows your breed of Angora rabbit to take part in the contest, you should go ahead and register your Angora rabbit.

Register your Angora rabbit in the show that you find relevant and suitable. You will be asked your name, your address, the breed, sex, age and color of your bunny. You might also be asked whether you have taken part in contests before. Once you have registered for the show, you need to make sure that you and the pet are ready. Make all the necessary arrangements to get to the venue before the final day in order to get your rabbit used to its surroundings.

After the Angora rabbit is registered to participate in the rabbit show, the wait for the final day begins. You have to ensure that you have all the necessary documents and a copy of the exact schedule with you. You should know the exact time when your bunny would be showed. Having these things handy will help you to avoid the last minute rush and tension.

While you are taking good care of the pet Angora and preparing well for the rabbit show, you should also prepare a handy kit. This kit will help you on the day of the show. Your kit should have all the items that the bunny or you might need on the final day of the show.

To begin with, you should securely keep the registration form of the Angora rabbit in the kit. You will need to show it at the venue. You should keep your business card with the form. Make sure that you keep a towel, some paper wipes, nail clippers and slicker brush. You can also keep scrap carpet square and hydrogen peroxide for emergency grooming and cleaning of the bunny. It is also a good idea to keep a collapsible stool. This will be essential when you know that chairs won't be available. You should also keep some fresh food and water for the bunny on the day of the show. Apart from packing the essentials for the Angora rabbit, don't forget to carry food and water for you.

2. On the day of the show

Rabbit shows will give you the opportunity not just to showcase your rabbit and win a potential prize; it will also help you to know other rabbit owners. These shows will allow you to the opportunity to widen your horizon and know more about your breed of rabbit and also the other breeds.

You will have to prepare all year round if you wish your rabbit to take participate in such shows. You will have to make sure that everything about the bunny is on point. While you have done your part for the preparation for the show, there are a few pointers that will help on the final day of the rabbit show.

You will be intimated about the time of the show and the time of judging the rabbits. You will also be assigned a pen by the organizers. You are supposed to keep the rabbit ready to be judged in the assigned pen. It is always better to reach the venue earlier. Once you reach the venue, look for the assigned pen for your bunny.

There is nothing much that you need to do from your side on the day of the show. It is advised to take the opportunity and observe other bunnies. You should relax and enjoy the show.

Even when the bunnies are being judged, there is not much that needs to be done. You should just make sure that the rabbit is in the pen at the time of judging. A bunny that is not in the pen will obviously not be judged. The process of the judging in a rabbit show is quite simple. The judges will visit all the pens and judge the bunnies on various parameters. If your Angora rabbit wins a prize, a card will be left by the judges on the pen your Angora rabbit. Once the entire process is over, you can take the card and get the equivalent prize money from the reception area.

Once you get your prize money, you are free to leave the rabbit show. You can also spend more time and connect with other owners. Irrespective of the result of the show, you should make sure that you make the most of this opportunity.

Conclusion

Thank you again for purchasing this book!

I hope this book was able to help you in understanding the various ways to domesticate and care for Angora rabbits.

Angora rabbits are cute, adorable, friendly and lovable animals. Even though they are loved as pets, there are still many doubts regarding domestication methods and techniques. There are many things that prospective owners don't understand about the animal. They find themselves getting confused as to what should be done and what should be avoided.

An Angora rabbit is a small and naughty animal that will keep you busy and entertained by all its unique antics and mischiefs. It is said that each animal is different from the other. Each one will have some traits that are unique to him. It is important to understand the traits that differentiate the bunny from other animals. You also have to be sure that you can provide for the animal, so it is important to be acquainted with the dos and don'ts of keeping the Angora rabbit.

Angora rabbits are very entertaining and lovable animals, but they should not be deprived of all that they would have found in their natural habitat. They have certain specific requirements that need to be met. You have to understand their specific requirements before you can decide to raise them.

If you are still contemplating whether you want to domesticate the Angora or not, then it becomes all the more important for you to understand everything regarding the pet. You can only make a wise decision when you are acquainted will all these and more. When you are planning to domesticate an Angora rabbit as a pet, you should lay special emphasis on learning about its behavior, habitat requirements, dietary requirements, breeding details and common health issues.

When you decide to domesticate an animal, it is important that you understand the animal and its species well. It is important to learn the basic nature and mannerisms of the animal. I hope this book helped you to equip yourself with this knowledge. If you already have an Angora rabbit, I hope this book helped you to strengthen your bond with your pet.

Thank you and good luck!

References

Note: at the time of printing, all the websites below were working. As the internet changes rapidly, some sites might no longer be live when you read this book. That is, of course, out of our control.

https://en.wikipedia.org

www.ehow.co.uk

http://www.runningbugfarm.com

http://joyofhandspinning.com

http://www.angorarabbits.co.za

http://www.rabbit.org

http://www.mnn.com

http://www.handallhousefarm.com

http://www.maineangoraproducers.com

http://twotalentshomestead.blogspot.in

http://www.raising-rabbits.com

http://www.angorafiber.com

https://joybileefarm.com

http://www.wikihow.com

https://www.thespruce.com

https://www.pets4homes.co.uk

http://www.hobbyfarms.com

www.bbc.co.uk

https://www.cuteness.com

www.training.ntwc.org

http://animaldiversity.org

https://a-z-animals.com

https://www.theguardian.com

http://www.businessinsider.com

https://hub.co-opinsurance.co.uk

https://www.popsugar.com

https://www.petcha.com

http://www.petrabbitinfo.com

https://www.peta2.com

CPSIA information can be obtained
at www.ICGtesting.com
Printed in the USA
LVOW10s1818031117
554902LV00010B/764/P

9 781788 650069